# DON'T LET THE ACCENT FOOL YOU

## The Journey of OIL EXPRESS Founder Art Lukowski from Stalin's Construction Camps to the Entrepreneur Hall of Fame

Arthur Lukowski and Albert Tyde

*Sharing Publishers*
Dyer, Indiana

**Sharing Publishers**
700 Roy Street
Dyer, IN  46311

Rewritten and Edited by Jeanine Harrison
Final Editing by Connie Lukowski
Cover Design, Interior Design and Production by Wayne E. Johnson

First printing 1997

Library of Congress Catalog Card Number: 97-66654

ISBN 0-9657522-0-8

Printed in the United States of America
10 9 8 7 6 5 4 3 2 1

*Art, whose true life story unfolds here, wishes to dedicate this book to his wife, Connie. Without her, the ending to this story wouldn't be the same. He wants to affirm that their children, Arthur Junior, Lisa, and Johnny were pure joy to him. They gave him the strength to go on in the most difficult times. Never in his life was there a moment when he didn't love them completely. He would like them to read this book, see the cultural differences between his childhood and theirs, and forgive him for any misunderstandings.*

*May his grandchildren read this book and praise this Country for her greatness.*

# Foreword

*To Dear Arlene Best wish and Enjoy my Book 11·23·99 Art Lukowski*

His story starts in Kiev, Russia, but it is as American as "Old Glory."

Oppressed in the old country, the immigrant comes to America for freedom and opportunity, as did millions before him. In a sense, he is "Everyman"; a metaphor for all of those who have gone before him and yet he is singular and unique because of the enormity of his victory over adversity. Incredibly, he succeeded against all odds. He hurdled the seemingly insurmountable obstacles of tragedy, tyranny, deprivation and incarceration to make his way to the United States.

Once here he found the freedom he sought and loves as only one who has lived without it can.

Once here he found the opportunity he sought and he used it for great good to found the hugely successful "Oil Express."

When Art Lukowski was presented with the Lifetime Achievement Award from the Entrepreneurship Hall of Fame, he said modestly, "If I could do it, anybody could do it." Really? How many of us could survive the suffering inflicted by the communists and the fascists? The father is executed. Mother and son nearly starve in slave labor camps. How many of us could come to Chicago with ten dollars, not speaking the language, knowing hardly anyone and go on to found and develop a multi-million dollar company like "Oil Express"?

Art Lukowski is no ordinary man. He is an inspiration to us all as a shining example of the American dream come true.

Jack Taylor, Principal Anchor
*Stock Market Observer*
WCIU-TV/Channel 26, Chicago

*Jack Taylor's career in radio an television news spans more than fifty years. He was a morning news reporter for WBBM-TV and principal anchor for the top-rated WGN-TV evening news. He has been in his current position with WCIU-TV since 1985.*

# Introduction

When I first set foot on American soil I realized it was the beginning of a new life for me. I had heard that there was no other country in the world which offered more opportunity and since I wanted to start and run my own business I knew it was the place for me. I had no idea just what that business would be, but it would be mine. I dreamed of how successful it would become, but I never imagined how many twists and turns my new American life would take—turns which eventually led me back to the Ukraine where my story actually begins.

It was the desire to record my life for my children and grandchildren that led to this book. I wanted them to know what things are possible in America no matter where you are from. Success will come as long as you are willing to work and learn and do more than is expected of you without worrying how you will be repaid.

As I began recording details I could see that it was important to not only tell of my early years in a Ukrainian construction camp from a child's viewpoint, but to document the historical events taking place outside my small world. The impact of these events—the purges of Stalin in the late 1930s which resulted in the disappearance of my father and the invasion of Hitler's armies—led me to where I am today.

There were good people who helped my mother and me through the difficult years in a German labor camp, after the war in DP camps in Europe, and after I came to America. These people offered me opportunities to work and to learn. There were other people with their own agendas who, perhaps because of my broken English, thought they could use me to get what they wanted—a stepping stone to where they wanted to go. From all of these people I learned lessons and skills which proved to be invaluable to me at some point in my life; from them I gained practical knowledge and experience which I used in building successful American businesses, culminating with Oil Express. Everyone who came into my life was a teacher and usually from the worst experiences came the most valuable lessons.

The end of the story, my trip to the Ukraine, is actually the beginning of a new story. After the fall of the Berlin wall and the break up of the Soviet Union the public was given access to long-classified Soviet documents. This allowed me to learn the fate of my father and enabled me to begin work on a permanent memorial to him and to the hundreds of thousands of other Ukrainian citizens who suffered a fate similar to his at the hands of Stalin.

This new story is yet unfinished.

—Arthur Lukowski

# KIEV

## The End and the Beginning

# Chapter 1

## The Beginning...

*"Mankind has not woven the web of life. We are but one thread within it. Whatever we do to the web, we do to ourselves. All things are bound together. All things connect."*

—*Chief Seattle, Suquamish leader and friend to settlers in the Northwest Territory*

I grasp my flowers tightly as I stand with the mayor of Kiev and other government officials in the shadow of the statue of the man. A ray of sunlight just touches his green copper head, eighteen feet or so above the ground—the head of a noble Ukrainian worker, hat in hands; and a cross. I glance out over the nearly two thousand visitors who have gathered for the dedication and memorial service. They are silent. The eight priests and two rabbis conducting the service have called for a moment of silent prayer.

Who is this Ukrainian worker? Who is this man whose likeness is reproduced here three times larger than life? Who is he that he could cause two thousand people to travel many miles or even like me from America, to a memorial service more than half a century after he died? Could he be my father who I last saw fifty years ago when he was taken away for questioning by the authorities? Who is he that this event would be televised nationally and covered by major newspapers?

All of us here know. He is part of us all, even the youngest who have only heard stories from grandmothers and grandfathers. To these young children they are just stories. But as they grow they will come to understand the truths in these stories—to understand why they were a part of this ceremony today.

I look down at the grass and soil beneath my feet; the soil of the country of my birth. I think of all that has happened to me and to my homeland in the sixty-eight years since I was born here in a Soviet construction camp near Kiev in the Ukraine.

My earliest memories began around age four. As a young child they were pleasant memories; soon-to-be short lived but pleasant, particularly the time I spent playing with Vania Molowany, a strapping private security guard with a gentle face. He would lift me up to the ceiling in his enormous hands and fly me through the air. This was the only life I knew—here in the construction camp. It was home. I was happy. I could not yet understand the events unfolding outside of my small world that would so drastically alter my life and the lives of my family members; or how my parents and brothers came to be there in the camp.

My father Joseph, of Latvian descent, was born in Obl. Kovencka Gubernia Rajon district, Tabelckij county, Klikoli village, Latvia, in 1892. As a civil engineer and officer in Tzar Nicholas II's Royal Army, he was stationed in Poland in 1914. It was here that he met my mother, Josephine Pokorski. She was a twenty-four-year-old widow from an arranged marriage.

*Joseph Lukowski*

Josephine and her young son Anatole lived on a pig farm with her eight brothers and sisters.

Early in Joseph's courtship of Josephine, Anatole fell off some battlements while playing and had to be hospitalized in Warsaw. When World War I raged closer to Warsaw, the hospital staff was forced to evacuate everyone to Kiev. Josephine followed her son and took a position as a waitress to support herself until Anatole was well. When Joseph discovered that Josephine was gone, he vowed to find her. He went to Kiev where he located her and asked her to be his partner for life. She accepted.

Anatole eventually recovered, and Joseph and Josephine had three sons together: Zan in 1918, Henry in 1923, and me, Arthur, on September 24, 1928. Unlike the other sons who managed to give my mother a six-year rest between births, I gave her only four. I had to. There was already sixteen years between me and Anatole and mother was thirty-eight. It was time.

Before going much farther, I should give you a brief history of the area up until my birth.

Life has never been easy for the people in Mother

Russia, a land of long, harsh winters and scant summers. Foreigners intent on conquest invaded—from the Mongols to Napoleon—followed by a succession of tzars who viewed the peasant population as serfs, born solely for service to the nobility.

The last of these tzars was Nicholas II who broadened his father's conservative stance through vast press censorship, heightened religious persecution, and restrictions on local assemblies. In 1917, because so many men had been conscripted to service in the Russian army, there was widespread famine; no one was left to plant and cultivate the fields. Two revolutions followed and Nicholas II abdicated his throne to the provisional Government, ushered in by the so-called February Revolution.

Ukrainian and Polish patriots rejoiced. They had dreamed of the day they would be free of the tyranny of the tzars; where music and singing were once again commonplace; where they could greet strangers and invite them in and exchange bread, vodka, and a bed for stories that would lighten their spirits and those of their children. Sadly, catastrophically, these hopes were never realized.

The provisional Government was weak because it had no common purpose. The government controlled the anti-Bolshevik White Army, made up of soldiers from the Royal Army of Nicholas II, monarchists, conservatives, liberals, Socialist revolutionaries, Mensheviks, and other political and social groups that rejected the idea of a totalitarian party. All were united to end the famine that had already killed five million people. The Bolshevik's Red Army, primarily under the leadership of Vladimir Ilyich Lenin, were communists who followed the teachings of Karl Marx. With Leon Trotsky leading the military, this Red Army saw the opportunity to seize control. During the resulting civil war which lasted from the summer of 1918 through April, 1920, Tzar Nicholas II and his family were murdered because Lenin feared that Nicholas might be rescued and inspire a counter-revolutionary movement. The Red Army was victorious; the White Army had no programs for after the war and therefore lacked the ability to recruit and empower troops. At the end of 1920, the communists were the masters of Russia.

World War I had been raging throughout Europe. Russia sided with France and Great Britain against Germany and Austria-Hungary to prevent their conquest of all of Europe. The German armies marched through Belgium and France. Poland and Russia became slaughter grounds for the stand-off between Germany and Russia. Russia was in the midst of the famine and entire regiments deserted.

Although the Russian effort came to a standstill, the Russian winter had taken its toll on the Germans. On March 3, 1918, Germany signed a treaty with the new Russian Communist Party in Brest-Litovsk and withdrew its troops, leaving behind devastation. Between 1917 and 1920 the combination of hunger and wars caused the death of approximately 17 million Russian citizens.

The reign of Lenin and Trotsky marked the beginning of a new and even more brutal totalitarian rule. Lenin, "Father of the Revolution," officially became Premier. Poets and other intellectuals either escaped or were banished to Siberia. The epicenter of people's lives became survival through silence because of the overwhelming fear of arrest, banishment or worse.

The Union of Soviet Socialist Republics (USSR), comprised of the Russian, Ukrainian, Byelorussian and Transcaucasion republics, was officially established at the end of 1922. The New Economic Policy had been instituted to stabilize the country and revitalize the economy by allowing farmers to lease land and sell their produce on the open market, and by allowing private ownership of factories and retail outlets.

Lenin died on January 21, 1924 as a result of paralysis

caused by a third stroke. In his honor Petrograd, the former Russian capital was renamed Leningrad. His death led to a battle for succession that was ultimately won by Joseph Stalin.

Lenin had come to realize that Stalin was dangerous and wrote a speech to discredit him. Lenin intended to deliver the public, personal attack on Stalin at the forthcoming Twelfth Party Congress. His third stroke, however, robbed him of his ability to speak. The draft of his speech was discovered by Stalin and destroyed.

# Chapter 2
# The Georgia Madman

*"A single death is a tragedy; a million deaths is a statistic."*

—*Joseph Stalin*

The "Great Father Stalin" was born into feudal system poverty as Iosif Vissarionovich Dzhugashvili in Gori, Georgia on December 21, 1879. There were questions whether his father was a domestic servant named Vissarion or a travelling general, Nikolai Przhvalsky. Since the young Stalin resembled the general somewhat, he was the more likely choice. His mother, Yekaterina, sent him to ecclesiastical schools and the seminary in Tiffis, hoping that he would become a priest. But sometime in his teens he moved from Orthodox Christianity to orthodox Marxism.

Joseph was a physically abused child who experienced periods of blind rage. During one of these periods he threw a knife at his father. He had lost respect for his mother, because he suspected her of infidelity. When she died he dishonored her by refusing to attend her funeral—a crime in Georgia. As an adult he assumed the name "Stalin" meaning "made from steel." And so it seemed he was—heart and soul. Georgians referred to Stalin as "kinto" which, in Georgian, means "sly crook." He was a bigot, hating his Georgians and neighboring Armenians equally and barely tolerating the Jews.

Post revolutionary days in the Soviet Union became increasingly tragic with the Bolsheviks continually tightening their political hold on vast, beautiful "Mother Russia." The year Henry was born and Lenin died was one not only of oppression, but also of the evaporation of Bolshevik morals. Churches that weren't burned were converted into stables. Holy icons were used for target practice. Stalin returned to "collectivization," again severing the farmers vital attachment to the land, leaving the fertile, black Ukrainian soil largely uncultivated.

Stalin proved to be more ruthless than any of the previous leaders or fellow communists. He reigned as dictator, his authority encompassing every aspect of society in the U.S.S.R. His dominion was characterized by three programs: collectivization, rapid industrialization, and great purges. The policies he created and implemented and his desire to eliminate his real or imagined opponents resulted in the incarceration and murder of millions of Soviet citizens.

After the revolution the communists replaced the tzar's double-headed black eagle symbol with the hammer and sickle. The hammer ridiculed the dilapidated and ancient industries; the sickle represented the backbreaking work performed daily by farmers, the people most persecuted by Stalin. To the people the hammer and sickle came to mean death and hunger: "Sierp i mlot, smierc i glod" was repeated over and over as people witnessed atrocities such as a bullet to someone's brain—or as they slowly died from hunger.

My brothers and I were born into this world.

# Chapter 3
## Boyhood Survival

*"The government believes that it pays good wages to its workers just as we, too, believe we are doing a good job for the government."*

—*Common, snide truism of Ukrainian forced laborers*

Near the end of World War I labor strikes in Russian territory crippled the country. The Germans withdrew, leaving behind destruction, hunger and desperation. My father's position allowed our family to survive more easily than most, but even so those times after the revolution and the war were ones of extreme duress. He was a member of the Communist Party from 1917 to 1920 and after he withdrew, worked for the government as a civil engineer, responsible for overseeing the building of roads and bridges in an approximate 100 to 120 kilometer radius of Kiev. Construction was carried out by forced laborers who lived in nearby camps and who received minimal compensation. Tardiness, absence, or reporting to work with vodka on one's breath meant exile to a labor camp or death. More than 100,000 kulaks ("fists"), the wealthier peasants who resisted because they had more to lose to collectivism, suffered this fate.

We lived in a Soviet construction camp near Kiev in the Ukraine. The base of the camp was a rectangle of approximately ten acres of elevated, sandy land surrounded by a nine-foot high green plank privacy fence. Four wooden guard towers, which also served as cramped living quarters for the guards, jutted upward from each corner. At the main gate stood a small guard house with windows facing the road and into the camp.

Our "home" was actually the main office which stood in the middle of the construction area, similar to the shelters in the typical Siberian prison camp. It had an elongated porch or deck which kept the sand on boots and feet from being carried into the house.

Along the left side of the camp by the railroad tracks were storage buildings which housed road building materials, trucks, tractors, heavy winter clothing for construction workers, tools and boots unloaded from the supply trains. Near these buildings was an open tar pit, about a half acre in size—a black mirror that reflected the sun. Scattered around the area were abandoned tractors, rusting away for lack of parts. Outhouses stood along the fence near the main gate.

Outside to the left of the main gate, a small turbulent creek had formed a fairly large pond. A short access road ran from the gate to a simple, wooden plank bridge over the creek and out to the main cobblestone road, a few yards away. Along the road nearby, a few houses on wooden stilts formed Darnica Village. If you looked toward the village on a clear day you could see the outline of Kiev in the distance. New Darnica stood just opposite the main gate and it was where my brothers and I attended school.

The majority of peasants resisted collectivization, an economic system based on the shared ownership and control of production and distribution. Collectivization caused the people to lose ownership and pride in their work. They destroyed their tools, burned their crops, and butchered and ate their livestock before they could be taken from them. A famine resulted, centering in the Ukraine, the northern Caucausus, and portions of Russia. The government closed its eyes to the situation while an estimated five to ten million peasants perished.

Fortunately for our family, mother managed to obtain bread, potatoes and a cow, which she kept hidden in a tool shed. The communist officials as well as the guards knew about the cow; officially she was counted as an addition to the road building equipment.

*One of the areas near the camp where Art played as a boy.*

She provided milk, geese in the camp provided eggs and the Bolsheviks provided some food for the workers and soldiers. All together, it was enough to sustain us.

Non-productive members of the population were not as fortunate. In the eyes of the commissars they were parasites. At one point during the famine I witnessed an old man in the road, picking up the waste from an Army horse. He wrapped it in a cloth and walked over to the creek where he washed away the waste and ate the remaining undigested grain.

The creek outside the main gate was about twelve feet in width at its widest point. The bridge, which sat close to the water, was strong enough to support supply vehicles. I spent many, countless hours on the bridge and in the tall wild grasses beside it, watching the fish and the fisherman trying to entice them onto their hooks.

One sunny day when I was six I stood on the bridge watching minnows in the creek below pass beneath me. I was startled as a tiny body, an infant, drifted out from under the bridge above the minnows.

"Quickly! You must come!" I called to the guard at the

main gate. "There is a baby in the water!"

The guard glanced in my direction and continued puffing on his "bumaha"— newspaper cigarette. He made no other move. I turned back to the stream and watched the baby float away until I could see it no more.

*A view of the creek from the bridge where the baby floated by.*

At one point along the stream there was an abandoned mill, another sign of the results of Soviet collectivism. To me it resembled a haunted house—and in a way it was. The stalls beside the mill had once held pigs; later, people. It was practical to raise pigs by the mill because they could be fed the hulls from the grain. But the hulls, brans and floor sweepings were gone—eaten by the desperately poor.

Days grew colder as winter approached. Late one of those chilly days I strolled along the road toward the camp with my mother. Crows circled overhead above the pines, their shrill caws calling others together to settle down for the evening. As we approached the bridge, my mother suddenly stopped. I looked up at her and I could see she was listening to something. Then I heard it, too. It was not the caw of a crow, but another sound—a low, moaning sound. We took another few slow, deliberate steps and there it was again—the moaning. It seemed to come from the tall grass at the water's edge near the bridge. My mother motioned for me to stay where I was, then she cautiously walked in the direction of the sounds. When she was about fifteen feet past the bridge, she called me over. There in the cold wet grass lay a wisp of a young woman, perhaps eighteen years old, nearly dead from starvation.

As fast as I could, I ran to the camp and found my soldier friend, Vania. I took him with me back to the creek where the young woman lay. He carefully picked her up and carried her back to our kitchen where he laid her gently on the table. She was so thin she almost looked transparent and seemed to be drifting in and out of a coma. My mother shooshed Vania and I out of the room and went to work washing the girl and checking her for lice. She finally wrapped her in a warm blanket and called us back in. Vania took her and placed her into one of our beds.

After a couple of days in my mother's care, the girl began to come around. She found her voice and was strong enough to tell us her story. Her name was Dasha and her village had been completely devastated by the Red Army. She told of how soldiers had searched the barns and houses, poking in the ground with long steel rods, looking for buried grain. Villagers who were not shot for hiding grain ran away, as she had done.

During her recovery Dasha spent hours entertaining me with stories of days past. Vania began to visit more often, too. He would sit with Dasha and hold her hand as he looked into her luminous, dark eyes. He gradually fell in love with her and she with him. When Dasha recovered completely she married her soldier. My family and I were overjoyed when they moved into a nearby cottage

In Russia, when a boy reached his eighteenth birthday, he was drafted into a branch of the Red military. Anatole, my oldest brother, was drafted into the Air Force and stationed at Dnepro-Petrovsk Base, about 200 miles southeast of Kiev. He was in training to be a co-pilot and had parachuted from altitudes over 20,000 feet. His progress was rapid so he was understandably shocked when orders came for him to be transferred to ground support. There was to be no more flying in his future. It seems that since his last name was Lukowski, not Lukovsky, he was considered a Polish national instead of a Russian national, and thereby suspect for having relatives in Latvia and Poland—a popular yet irrational aspect of the Soviet mentality.

Anatole's spirits fell. His new assignment was as a chauffeur for the Air Force. On official trips to Kiev, he occasionally had the opportunity to stop back home and visit. I was exhilarated whenever he returned because he'd let me sit on his lap and steer his military vehicle around the yard while he pushed the pedals and shifted gears.

Children in Russia were given nicknames by their parents. Mother and father aptly nicknamed me Turek, meaning "one with an independent spirit who learns by experimenting." As a six-year-old I was in awe of anything with a motor and a hum. The shiny, black 1930 Ford that Anatole chauffeured seemed to me to have a life of its own with a skittish, cantankerous nature with headlight "eyeballs" peering mischievously around the radiator. My interest in the vehicle eventually got me into trouble

Anatole had come for one of his visits and left the car in the yard with the key in the ignition. I spotted it and decided to do a more thorough exploration than I had a chance to do when Anatole was with me. I climbed in and pretended I was driving. The next step was to switch on the ignition. I became more daring and started shifting the gears and playing with different controls. The windshield wiper swooshed back and forth and the starter cranked away. I discovered a control on the dashboard which made the car initially lurch forward and slowly roll ahead. This was wonderful to me. I discovered that by keeping one hand on the starter button and the other on the steering wheel, I could drive in circles around the yard.

The guards observed my antics and practically doubled over with laughter. Eventually the car ran slower and slower until it finally stopped. The accumulator, as Russians called the battery, had died. It was then that I saw my mother standing in our doorway. The anger slowly distorted her face as she realized just what I had been up to. She bolted from the house and yanked me out of the auto by the arm. It was then that I received my first good spanking.

I had no toys to play with in the camp, so much of my playtime was spent on the rusting tractors in the sheds. I imagined myself driving them through the villages and towns of the Ukraine. Many times I had driven through Kiev in my mind and that one, real experience of driving alone in Anatole's car was exhilarating. A spanking was a small price to pay for such a thrill.

One afternoon I was amusing myself by watching white geese parade along the green camp fence as I stood on the office porch. I liked seeing them stop just long enough to nibble on stubborn weeds that had grown underneath.

"Art!" I turned in the direction of the main gate. It was a friend of mine calling to me. "Come see what I found!"

I hurried over to him. He led me to an elevated shed. There, underneath, was the body of a boy of about twelve. My friend bent down an touched one of the decomposing arms. A watery fluid oozed out. We both knew that he, like many others, was a victim of starvation. The fluid was excess water he had drunk to ease the cramps and fill his hollow stomach.

In a few hours some police arrived to carry away the boy's body. There would be no investigation, though. This was routine, a daily occurrence.

Soon after, changes began taking place in the camp. A platoon of soldiers were stationed near the base, where they worked day and night leveling the ground, spreading gravel and constructing wooden barracks. A few days after the barracks were completed, a column of tanks approached and

**Kiev**

stopped by the new barracks.

I had been watching all of this with great interest through the slots in the green camp fence. I had never seen so many tanks in my life. I made up my mind that one day I would become a tankist and wear one of the warm wool hats with ear flaps that could be pulled down, just like the ones these soldiers wore.

It was wonderful to stand by the fence and listen to the soldiers sing and harmonize as they made their way to the kitchen for meals. The smooth blends of tenors and baritones were enhanced by their crescendos. Their singing gave me goosebumps.

One of my favorite songs was a popular one which when translated meant:

*Apples and pear trees are in blossom,*
*The river's captured by misty waves,*
*Katyusha roamed along the river,*
*Steep and high there was a bank,*
*She used to roam and sing along,*
*All about the steppe greyish eagle,*
*All about the one to whom she was devoted,*
*And whose letters she dearly kept.*

# Chapter 4
# A New Home

*"We have knowledge of socialism,
but as for knowledge of…the
organization and distribution of
commodities—that we have not.
This the old Bolshevik leaders did
not teach us…."*

—*Vladimir Ilyich Lenin*

When I was seven, our family was informed that we would be leaving the construction camp. All military bases were cloaked in secrecy and the civilians in the camp lived too close to the base for their comfort. Everyone had to move out to nearby Darnica.

On the day before our move, I stood at my favorite spot on the bridge, thinking about how my life would be changing, when a small funeral procession approached on the cobblestone road. A simple casket was carried by six pall-bearers. In front of them were two women, loudly weeping and crying. Their shrill laments pierced through the quiet of the area. I was disturbed. Why are they crying so loudly, I wondered. People all over were starving and no one was crying for them. I thought about the tiny baby I had seen in the stream. Little children were dying and no one was crying for them. Why all this commotion for one person in a casket? I didn't know it then, but this was a Jewish funeral and, as was their custom, the two women were professionals who had been hired to cry for money.

Moving day arrived. Our new home was surrounded by pine trees with one so close that it scraped the straw-covered roof. Six compact apartments had been hastily constructed inside. Some doorways had boards or shaggy blankets covering them to muffle the sounds from the next apartment.

Our three-room apartment had a kitchen with a small storage pantry and a wood-burning stove with a sheet metal flue. The stove was used for cooking and was the only source of heat in the winter. A second cramped room was a bedroom for my two brothers and me. The last room was only slightly larger and served as a living room, dining room and bedroom for my parents. Two outhouses, one for men and one for women stood off a small distance behind the house. Toilet paper was not available, but the Soviet newspaper *Pravda* proved most suitable for this purpose.

Indoor plumbing was not an option. Water from the stream served the people of the village in the spring, summer, and fall. In winter it froze over. My mother paid very close attention to the cleanliness of our family. All the women washed clothes by boiling them first to prevent the spread of lice. The soap we were given was foul-smelling and very limited in quantity; sometimes we had none.

This year, before winter set in, construction men on horse-drawn wagons delivered concrete cylinders five feet in diameter and six feet in length for the people of the village to build a well. Many people helped unload the tubes. After much discussion as to the proper location for the well, one of the cylinders was placed on end at the agreed-upon spot. A worker with a shovel and a bucket jumped up and disappeared inside the cylinder.

I wondered what was going on in there. Soon I saw the bucket appear at the top edge. Another worker grabbed it and walked to a small pine grove where he emptied it. As they continued the process, what I could see of the cylinder became less and less, sinking into the ground under its own weight as the earth was removed from beneath it. When just the top of the rim was showing, workers placed another cylinder on top of the one in the ground.

I watched for several days, losing count of how many cylinders were eventually stacked in the hole. Finally one day the digging stopped. The men installed a pulley, long rope and bucket atop the well. All the villagers came and brought vodka to celebrate the completion of their new community well.

As the winter approached, I would occasionally walk back to the abandoned construction camp, my first home. On each visit, it was more dilapidated. Anything that could be scavenged was, particularly wood. Only the skeletons of the sheds and guard towers remained, their skins stripped for firewood.

Winter was not a comfortable time for anyone in Darnica. One Russian aptly stated, "We have here a good climate. The winter is only nine months long and the rest is all summer." As schoolchildren, we had to walk two miles to the school, then walk two miles back home regardless of the weather. The concern of our mothers for our warmth and protection from the effects of Father Frost transformed us from children into bulky woolen bundles with eyes. Often we would be accompanied by an elderly villager with a long wooden stick, used for waving off any hungry wolves that would venture out of the forest. The wolves posed a great danger for children. Occasionally a child playing near the forest would disappear.

In spite of everything, that winter was one of the happiest for me. My mother had taken my winter shoes to the shoemaker to have him install a special metal plate on the sole of each shoe. With just a small wrench I could attach ice skating blades to the plates and become one of the few children who could skate on the frozen road beside the creek all the way to school. Not only did skating reduce my travel time, but it was also fun. Everything along my route became a part of a winter wonderland. "Hey, Georgia!" "Hey, Ivan!" I would call out as I went gliding past all of the other children walking on the path to school.

*Joseph Lukowski (second from right) and associates on one of their completed bridges.*

I did miss my father. His job as a civil engineer kept him away much of the time. We were lucky if we saw him once a week. One cold evening we anxiously awaited his arrival. The time grew late and he did not appear. My mother became more uneasy with each passing hour. Finally we heard some noise outside. The door opened and there stood my father. His car had broken down and he had to find a farmer with a team of oxen willing to tow his car the remaining ten miles of the trip home.

One of the greatest career accomplishments of Comrade Joseph Lukowski, Civil Engineer was the supervision of the construction of a bridge which spanned the Dnieper River, close to Kiev. It was an unusual bridge, constructed from massive chains. The riverbed beneath was very soft and the pilings had to be placed very deep; so soft that it was necessary to completely divert the river to erect the bridge. A few other engineers had attempted to finish the bridge and had failed before my father was brought in to oversee the project. He managed to complete the project on time and received a Certificate of Merit and a gift directly from Joseph Stalin. The gift was a granite desk set with two ink wells, one for black ink and the other for red, with a place for a pen in between. On the face of the granite was a hammer and sickle with an inscription from "Bactchko (Father) Stalin."

I was immensely proud of my father and used every opportunity to boast of his accomplishment and his granite reward to my friends. Their fathers had never received such an acknowledgment.

The following summer my father was assigned to an even more distant project, one which would make even the occasional weekend trips home impossible because of the adverse, unpredictable road conditions. Our family made a quick decision to move closer to the project. We loaded all of our possessions into the car, boarded up the apartment, and headed east to a village near Malin.

As we drove through the village, some of the villagers panicked. They had never seen an automobile before and were afraid this noisy, smoky, black machine might explode. They ran to the well to get buckets of water which they placed in front of their doors just as a precaution.

Our new home was a typical Ukrainian village house constructed a rough timber frame, plastered with a mixture of common clay and short cut straw. The walls were white-washed with hydrated lime paste. The roof was made from sticks covered with a layer of rye straw with steep gables to shed the heavy winter snow. Inside, a large clay and stone baker's hearth took up most of the main room. It was about five feet high, designed to burn very long logs, with room enough to bake large loaves of bread or roast a whole pig or goat. It was designed to retain heat throughout the night. Shelves built along the sides served as beds during cold win-ter nights to keep a family warm even when temperatures dropped well below zero.

When the weather was pleasant, my father let me trav-el with him to various construction sites in the area. The wooden bridges there were being built by forced laborers from labor camps—"slave workers." Most of these workers were "convicts," enemies of the state and other "non-produc-tives"—artists or philosophers whose influence Stalin feared.

The labor camps served a dual purpose for Stalin. They provided a source of cheap labor while ridding the country of political "criminals," who could be exterminated by being worked to death. The least fortunate were sent to Siberia where even some forms of wildlife could not survive. They slaved in the impossible conditions and died by the thousands from hunger and cold. Even those in the labor camps were lucky to survive six months. "Rule by fear" was Stalin's motto.

On one trip with my father to a remote area, I wan-dered off with a small pail to entertain myself by picking wild berries. I bent over to pick a few that were low-growing. When I straightened up I was staring directly into the eyes of a timber wolf. The two of us froze for what seemed like an eternity—not moving, not breathing, just staring. I finally dropped my pail, turned and ran. The wolf took off just as quickly in the opposite direction.

When I reached the construction office, I told my father what had happened. He sat me on his knee and told me the story of his encounter with wolves.

Several years back he was walking through the forest on his way home from work. Gradually he became aware that he was not alone. He turned slowly and saw a pack of wolves stalking him a short distance away. They worked their way around the trees, moving closer and closer. Joseph knew they would attack when the moment was right. He picked a nearby tree and climbed as quickly as he could. The wolves bounded in, surrounded the tree, and began gnawing on the bark.

Twilight approached and my mother began to get worried because by now my father was usually home. She summoned a few of the villagers to come with her along the path that my father always followed. They lit their lanterns and hurried off. As they approached the tree my father had used to save himself, light from the lanterns scared the wolves away, further into the forest. Much of the bark of the tree had been eaten away, but he was safe.

As I got older, I held my father in higher regard as was customary for Ukrainian boys. I grew closer to Henry, my brother closest in age to me. He was both my protector and partner in crime. The Communists attempted to destroy family bonds by shifting the focus from the family to the government, making devotion to the State the highest priority for an individual. Teachers asked schoolchildren to spy on their parents and report any suspicious activity or conversations against the State back to them

*Henry Lukowski*

so the teachers could notify the authorities. The parents would then be brought in for "questioning." Stalin was to be considered their real father, the one who looked out for the welfare of all. Many parents lived in fear of their own young children.

We were taught that there was no God. People were arrested and would disappear for even speaking of Him. The greatest sin was a bad deed against the State. Yet, in spite of all this, my mother had each one of us baptized behind locked doors. At one point she gave my oldest brother Zan a holy card with a prayer on it dated 1899, from when she was a girl in Poland. He kept it for years in a secret compartment inside his wallet.

Some children were perceptive enough to read between the lines of this propaganda and not reveal anything that went on within the family. I was one of these children. I lived in fear that one day something bad would happen to my parents.

Since there was no Christmas, the New Year's celebration brought presents for the children and provided a bright spot in the long dark winter. After that, our thoughts turned daydreams of the flowering green of Spring, soccer and summer fun.

I was always intrigued by the pond close to the town, mostly because my father had forbidden me to go near it. As a nine-year-old it became easier for me to bend a few rules for the sake of having fun and feeling alive. So one day when my friends wanted to play by the pond, I could no longer see any harm to it. I went with them.

As luck would have it, my father happened to drive by and see me there. He held his fist up out of the car window and shook it at me. I didn't know what this would mean, but I got a terrible ache in my heart. I had disappointed my father whom I loved and respected.

Disobedience also meant punishment although I wasn't sure what it would be because I'd never seen my father discipline my older brothers. When necessary, he would call the disobedient son into his room. There was no yelling or screaming or sounds of paddling—only a lot of weeping when the son returned. My brothers never discussed what took place. I had no idea what to expect. Would it hurt? If it did, how much?

That evening, my father returned home from work, ate his dinner as usual, and sat and read the newspaper. I dreaded each new minute as it arrived. At last my father calmly laid his newspaper aside, stood, and called me into the adjoining room. With downcast eyes and spirits, I went to him.

"Sit, please, Arthur."

I obeyed.

"Do you know why I asked you not to go near the pond?"

I shook my head no.

"The sluice that is there across the stream; it forms the pond. Because it obstructs the flow of water it also catches much debris...including the bodies of starved people floating down the little river...especially in the spring."

I understood my father's reasoning. Because he knew there was not much for a young boy to do at the camp, he could not be too angry with me for being curious.

I left the room relieved and I never loved him more than I did at that moment.

That summer was a good one for me. Anatole had finished his military tour and was employed as a driver for a government construction company. He had a car available to him on Sundays and he would take me with him on his dates with his girlfriend, Hala. Anatole would sometimes drive us to a picturesque spot for a picnic. Hala would entertain by playing songs for us on her balalaika. I loved her as much as I did my brother because she was gentle and kind and sweet to me.

Some Sundays Anatole would take me along to visit his good friend, Vasily. Vasily was a forest ranger living with his family in a remote area of the country. They had an expansive vegetable garden and a wonderful root cellar filled with cucumbers, green and red tomatoes, beets, potatoes, and cabbage. Vasily was fortunate that his mother-in-law was a sister to the Commissar of War, Voroshilov, who had replaced Leon Trotsky. Vasily's family was able to produce and keep food which was in such short supply everywhere. Vasily himself was very generous in nature and would send a basket of fruit and vegetables home with Anatole and me at the end of each visit. This afforded me the opportunity to try for the first time sauerkraut with oil, sprinkled with sugar—a very old Ukrainian dish.

Food was not the only item in short supply. Even products supposedly available to the general populous were hard to obtain. My mother had a friend who was a salesperson in one of the government stores, and she would let her know ahead of time when a shipment of, say, sugar would be due in the following day. Everyone would then be allowed to buy a limited amount, such as four pounds. Whenever one was privy to such news, one knew never to wait for tomorrow. Mother took Zan, Henry and me with her to the shop the night before to take our place in the line. We would wait all night to be there first when the shop opened in the morning.

One day mother received news that we would be visited by Vasily's son, Feodor, a well-connected party member and nephew of Commissar Voroshilov. Feodor was an officer in the Red Air Force and would be an honored guest. Mother began planning a very special dinner for the occasion. It would be a difficult task—not the preparation, but shopping for the goods. Mother decided that I would be her helper.

All shops in the Soviet Union were inefficiently run government operations. Many times Red Party workers stole the best merchandise and sold only what remained. Although only three percent of the people belonged to the Party, they controlled the operations and could do as they wished without fear of penalty.

The store we were required to use was divided into three sections: Baked Goods, Milk and Eggs; Canned and Packaged Food; and Meat. We had to stand in lines everywhere. The first was outside long before the store opened and after the Party workers finished their breakfast—ten or fifteen minutes late. Then we would each go to a different section of the store and stand in line to make our selections at the counter, where the woman would give us a receipt. We would then take the receipt and go stand in line for the cashier where we would pay for the goods. Once we had our stamped receipts we would take them back to the sections where we had made our selections and trade the receipts for the goods. The stores closed for an hour at lunchtime. All customers were hustled outside whether they had finished shopping or not, regardless of the weather.

Customers were also required to provide their own bags. Everyone carried a thin mesh bag in his or her pocket or purse. In case the opportunity to make a purchase presented itself, you would have a readily available means of carrying your items.

Mother was exhausted from our shopping as we began the long walk home. When we came near the house, we noticed a single engine airplane flying very low, "buzzing" our house and doing Dutch rolls. Zan and Henry ran outside and I ran to meet them. The pilot was Feodor, our dinner guest. Feodor deftly executed two chandelles, then flew off in the direction of Boryspol Airport, about fifteen miles away.

While I scurried around the neighborhood bragging to my friends about the "big shot" air force officer flying overhead who would soon be sitting at our dinner table, mother busied herself with preparation of the meal from what had been made available to us that morning. In a couple of hours Anatole arrived with Feodor who greeted my mother with a large bouquet of flowers from the Crimea on the Black Sea, the U.S.S.R.'s equivalent to Florida.

Following the lovely meal, father and the young men sat around the table visiting while Henry and I helped mother clean up the dishes. With a final compliment to mother on her excellent dinner, Anatole and Feodor excused themselves. They were on their way to Kiev to finish the evening with Hala and Feodor's girlfriend. As he departed, Feodor gave me a pin—Red Air Force wings. Right then I changed my mind and chose to be a "pilotchik" instead of a tankist when I grew up.

I lay awake in bed that night, too excited to sleep. I couldn't wait to show off my new pilot's wings to my friends and to tell them all about Feodor. I was exhilarated.

Then I heard violent pounding on the front door.

# Chapter 5
# A Family Tragedy

*"By lifting their hands against
Comrade Stalin, they lifted them
against all the best that humanity
possesses. For Stalin is hope; he is
expectation; he is the beacon that
guides all progressive mankind."*

—*Condemnation of the
victims of Stalin's terror by
Nikita Krushchev*

I held my breath and listened.

"Who is there?" my father called out.

"The police. We are here to check your passport!"
came the loud response.

"Under the constitution, citizens are not to be disturbed between midnight and 6:00 a.m.," father shouted back.

"Forget the constitution! Open the door or it will be
broken down!"

I climbed out of bed and peeked out into the room.
Father opened the door slightly. It was thrown open the rest
of the way and one officer and nine soldiers barged in, taking
positions in different parts of the house. Some stood, some
sat; all had rifles and bayonets at the ready. Mother was petri-
fied and covered her face with her hands. The soldiers wore
soiled uniforms with ankle-length coats. Only the officer had
a clean uniform.

From that point everything happened so quickly it
seemed surreal to me.

"Dress," the officer instructed my father. "You will

come with us for questioning—two, maybe three days."

While father readied himself, the officer turned to mother. "Don't worry. Your husband will be home soon. You need only pack a couple changes of underclothes. He will need nothing more for his short absence."

Mother obeyed, hurriedly putting father's underclothes in a small sack.

"What am I to be questioned about?" asked father as he put on his coat.

"I am not the examiner," the officer replied.

While mother finished packing the small sack, Zan and Henry each had a brief moment with father. Impatiently, a soldier grabbed the bag from mother and roughly pushed father through the door. I ran out of my room after father, but a soldier stood in the doorway. He blocked me with his bayonetted rifle. Neither mother nor I had a chance to hug him or kiss him or bid him farewell. It was the last time I ever saw him.

The officer and some soldiers remained, going through every book, every album, page by page. None of us knew what they were searching for. We were told to sit in one place or else wait outside.

We sat motionless like statues while they ransacked our home. They dumped out all the drawers. They ripped pillowcases. They cut open the mattresses.

The soldiers smoked cigarettes made from homegrown tobacco carried in a trouser pocket and rolled in newspaper. The house was filled with smoke and the foul stench of the soldiers.

At around 6:00 am they finally left, taking with them 44 of our photographs and fifteen documents. Before they left mother pleaded with the officer to take the certificate and plaque my father had personally received from Stalin, thinking it might help him.

"It means nothing," the officer said and slammed the door.

My mother went to the window and looked out. She let out a cry of terror when she saw what was outside.

The soldiers had brought the Vorona, the "crow," a hellish vehicle for the transportation of prisoners. It was constructed with four compartments to hold one prisoner in each in such a way that the prisoners could neither stand nor sit—only kneel. The chambers were even more torturous when the vehicle was in motion. It was felt that by the time prisoners reached their destination, they would already be partially broken and less likely to resist. Father had been outside in the Verona for hours since he was taken from the house. The vehicle started up and headed in the direction of Kiev.

That day our house was filled with shock and grief. Why had father been taken? He was not politically minded. Perhaps that was it. At one time he had been a party member but after three years decided not to continue his membership. He felt that he would rather do his best for the party as a construction engineer.

But we knew of Stalin's ruthlessness. Mother was beside herself. She thought that if only he had accepted and become a party member, this wouldn't have happened. Then she questioned if even that would have protected him since Stalin's purge spread to party members as well. She blamed Anatole, thinking that if he had been home with Feodor instead of dancing with the girls, Feodor's connection to the Commissar of War may have helped.

Mother took to her bed, overwhelmed by the events of the night and early morning. She cried constantly. Zan took over her responsibilities of cooking. No one wanted to eat. He brewed tea, but no one wanted to drink. When one of us tried to get mother to eat she would only plead, "Just leave me alone."

She went on like that for three days. We finally got her up by telling her about our two family dogs. They had been refusing food and water and we thought someone might have poisoned them. Mother got herself together enough to take the dogs to the veterinarian. He examined them, but could find nothing physically wrong. He felt that they, too, were suffering from grief. A short time later they both died.

The arrest of Joseph Lukowski had, unofficially, made him an enemy of the state. As members of his family, we were enemies as well. Except for dear Vania and Dasha, everyone severed ties with our family so they might not suffer a similar fate.

Zan was attending an institution of higher learning and while there he got the idea of gathering signatures on a petition asking for the release of father. Zan managed to obtain six pages of signatures which he sent to the general prosecutor in Moscow.

We received a response from the General Prosecutor. It was dated March 24, 1938 and stated, "Your petition is turned over to the Ukrainian prosecutor's office. There is where you should inquire." A glimmer of hope.

*The General Prosecutor's response*

*Notification from the Office of the Prosecutor in Kiev*

Some time later we received another letter, this one from the Office of the Prosecutor in the city of Kiev. "We received your petition and it will be reviewed."

That was the last word we ever had.

We kept watching the lists of arrested people in the newspaper. The name of Joseph Lukowski never appeared. Zan would also visit the prison in Kiev to bring father fresh underwear. The guards at the gate would always accept the package but never allow Zan inside.

Mother became increasingly bitter and sank further into depression. She rarely showed affection for any of us anymore. Finally, on one of Zan's prison visits several months after father's arrest, a guard told him, "Don't return. The court sentenced you father to ten years in Siberia without communication."

Papers were sent to our home explaining that father had been found guilty of sabotage for building a highway six inches too wide, thereby wasting the State's manpower and materials.

**Kiev**

Our house was half a mile from a major train crossing in Darnica. Many times I had seen trains pass with cattle cars full people being sent to Siberia—sometimes three in a week. Zan made up a two-foot by six-foot sign with LUKOWSKI printed on it in large letters and went to the train crossing, where he joined the fifteen or twenty other people with signs. Some had two or three signs they carried for members of other families that could not be there. The trains ran on no set schedule and sometimes there were very long waits. When a train would pass, the people waiting would hold up their signs for the prisoners to see. The idea was that if any of the men on the train knew the fate of the person on the sign, he would shout it out. But for our family the answer was always the same: "No."

Sometimes the prisoners would manage to write their names on small pieces of paper and toss them from the train, hoping that someone would pick up the papers and inform their families that they were being sent away. Mother always managed to pick up some of the notes to pass along, and invariably they contained the same thing: a name and address, a loving goodbye, and a brief message stating that they had been sentenced to Siberia for ten years—always ten years.

No one knew for sure how many prisoners were in a cattle car. Some thought forty, but there were times when we could see them packed like sardines with standing room only. Each train was a caravan of 65 to 75 cars. If, on the conservative side, each car contained only forty people, that would mean 2,600 people were being exiled to Siberia three times every week. If the "sardine" estimate was more accurate, it would be more in the range of 13,000 three times per week in cars with no toilet facilities—only piles of straw on the floors, replaced every so often on the outskirts of a town along the way. Travel time to Siberia was three weeks.

These arrests and expulsions aided Stalin in three ways. First, they frightened the populous into submission.

Second, they gave the State free labor in Siberia to mine gold, silver and coal, and for harvesting the forest. Third, there was more housing, food and jobs left for those citizens remaining in the cities.

The State provided the prisoners with saws, hammers and oxen; they were forced to build their own shelters from the raw materials they found there. Some prisoners working the mines lasted two or three years. Others, such as doctors or engineers with less labor-intensive jobs and better food and quarters, could survive longer

It has been estimated that 20 million people were sent to Siberia. Alexander Solzhenitsyn, a Nobel Prize Laureate in literature, claims the number was closer to 40 million. He himself miraculously endured ten years there. He was arrested by the Soviet armed forces counter intelligence agency SMERSH while a captain in the Red Army for having made derogatory remarks about Stalin to a school friend.

We had to get on with our lives as best we could and keep the hope alive that father would be one of the survivors. Mother found work as a packer in a chocolate factory in Kiev. Henry and I attended to the house. We tried to be as considerate as possible to mother in her fragile emotional state even though some of her actions were difficult for us to understand.

We were not allowed to play music on the radio or even to laugh. Mother would inquire accusingly, "How can you be happy with your father probably cold and hungry in Siberia?" Each summer for father she would prepare about three gallons of strawberry preserves thinking that, should he return, she would nurse him back to health with preserves and tea. The preserves were her top priority. She would spend her last kopaieks (pennies) on strawberries instead of on food for us.

And we kept visiting the railroad crossing, holding up our sign.

# Chapter 6

# The Great Escape

*"Do not do what you would undo if caught."*

—*Leah Arendt*

Vania had now attained a government position as a caretaker of horses and buggies. When summer came, he and Dasha purchased two little goats, about eight pounds each. Vania told mother that once the goats had offspring, she would have them as a source of milk for her family. That is how I ended up as caretaker for several goats that proved to be lifesavers for us.

The goats were kept in a 10' by 10' pen beneath the house of Vania and Dasha. It was my responsibility to take them out to a nearby pasture to graze. I would then milk them and put them back in their pen. I also had my own hidden agenda. Mother had forbidden Henry and me to swim in the stream unsupervised, fearing that we might drown. So I used the grazing goats as an opportunity to get near the stream for a quick swim—keeping one eye on the goats all the while.

Zan had begun to wear three "hats." He served as a salesman for a streetcar line, selling tickets to conductors to pass on to passengers. He had moved to Kiev and was, by night, still a student. While he was at home and mother was working, Zan was in charge of Henry and me—and he became a very strict "father," with permission from mother to whip us if he deemed it necessary. Swimming was one of those actions which she deemed deserving of a whipping.

Of course, the fear of a whipping did not stop us—it only made swimming more of an adventure. While the two of us were in the water, we would watch for the train from Kiev that carried mother home from the chocolate factory. As soon as we saw it we would get dressed and run like the devil to beat her home. She could always tell, though, if we had been in the water and if Zan was unavailable, she'd whip us herself with a rubber hose.

I feared the wrath of both Zan and mother. However, I was also headstrong and, I felt, clever. I liked to take "vacation" days from school when it was warm and sunny. I would hitch a ride on a passing train and jump off a few miles down the road to go birdwatching in the forests around Kiev. I had my collection of birds' eggs in nests and I sat enthralled watching songbirds build and tend to their nests and give nourishment to their young. It was much better than sitting confined in a classroom.

I'd begun taking so many holidays that notices from school arrived in the mail. Since Henry and I arrived home before mother, the notices never seemed to find their way into her hands.

One afternoon, though, the postman brought a letter from school. When I reached for it, he pointed out that it was registered and only Josephine Lukowski could sign for it. He said he would return later that evening to make certain she received it.

I was overtaken by panic. I could already feel the smart of the rubber hose and mother's impenetrable look of scorn, so I came up with a desperate plan.

Our family doctor had once told me that if I ever had a pain in my right side I must come to see him at once. That bit of advice was all I needed to develop a horrific, stabbing pain in my right side—so severe that I had to hurry to the hospital Emergency Room, moaning and groaning. The doctor didn't want to take any chances, so he took me into surgery to perform an appendectomy. At that time, young children given general anesthesia were at great risk, so I was given a shot in the side to numb the area locally. Sandbags were placed on my stomach to make my side bulge out. I watched all the preparations in a nearby mirror, but as the doctor began the incision, I fainted.

I didn't awaken until the next morning. The first thing that I saw was my mother's face awash with sympathy for her poor, sick boy. She also brought candy to help cheer me up. After ten days recovery at home I returned to school, a bit wiser. By the end of the school year I managed to improve my attendance and pull my grades up to A's. Even though I had learned a rather painful lesson, I was still proud of my "great escape."

# Chapter 7
# German Friendship

*"The national government...will take
under its firm protection Christianity
as the basis of our morality, and the
family as the nucleus of our nation...
Germany must not and will not sink
into Communist anarchy."*

—*Adolph Hitler*

By the mid-1930s it was apparent to Stalin that the rising anticommunist dictator Adolph Hitler was becoming a force to be reckoned with. Stalin increased his efforts to improve relations with both his neighbors in Eastern Europe and the West. However, by 1938 he became frustrated with his lack of success, so he switched tactics: He decided to do some politicking towards Hitler, hoping to maneuver to some middle ground between the two regimes. Hitler's expansion was very visible and any peace seemed more distant each day.

On August 23, 1939, the Soviet Union and Germany signed the ten-year non-aggression Molotov-Ribbentrop pact. It contained a promise of neutrality between the two nations, as well as a "secret protocol" that divided Poland between them and assigned spheres of authority in the Baltic region.

It was surmised that Stalin signed the agreement to stall for additional time to muster his troops. His forces had been drastically downsized due to his own purges; and those who remained were largely incompetent. He hoped to sit on the sidelines and watch the Western Allies and Germany eliminate each other, leaving the U.S.S.R. in control.

Stalin knew that Hitler needed his raw materials. But he was unaware that Hitler was already forming his own plan for the future of the U.S.S.R.

On September 1, 1939, the German armies attacked Poland from the west. When Stalin saw Poland failing in its attempts to resist the German onslaught, the Soviet armies invaded Poland from the east.

After the tyrants were victorious, they professed great affection, friendship and admiration for each other by way of telegrams. In one, Stalin said to Hitler that their friendship was "sealed in blood—Polish blood."

We had no way of knowing the true political situation of that time, though, foreign or domestic. Our news came via the *Pravda*, which means "truth." Of course the only truth in *Pravda* was the name—the government remained the keeper of the real truth.

Train movement around Kiev had increased dramatically. Steaming locomotives sped boxcars loaded with grain and other commodities to the west to aid Hitler's forces. Train after train after train loaded with human cargo still headed east to Siberia in a continuous, single file line of cattle cars.

Once in a while one of the trains would stand idle for a short time at the depot in Darnica and I could get close enough to have a brief conversation with some of the condemned. I learned they were citizens of Polish descent mostly, but also a good number of them were Estonians, Lithuanians and Latvians.

One Sunday, while my brothers and I were in the house, my mother placed some rubles in the middle of the table. "You boys go th the movies today and I will rest a bit." We were shocked by her uncharacteristic offer, but that quickly passed. We grabbed the money, got ourselves ready and left before she changed her mind.

The three of us had not gone more than a few hundred yards when Zan, who had been absorbed in thought, stopped suddenly. Henry and I turned to him.

"Something is wrong with our mother!" he said. "She does not even let us sing, and here she sends us to see a funny movie? No, something is wrong!"

The three of us turned and headed back. Zan became filled with a sense of urgency and began running. Henry and I did our best to try and keep up.

Zan ran into the house first. "Mother! Mother!" he called as he hurried through the small rooms. Then he saw her. She was hanging by her neck inside the big wardrobe cabinet. Frantically, Zan grabbed a kitchen knife. He cut her down and began working on her mouth and chest to make her breathe again. Thank God he succeeded.

Once she started coming around, the reality of the situation began to set in. The three of us began to cry to think that she would willingly leave us orphans, as far as we knew, unprotected in a stark, sometimes cruel world.

"Matushka, why did you do it? We love you," cried Zan.

"We do not have our father. Now you want to go away, leaving us alone here as orphans!" sobbed Henry.

We continued our entreaties for the rest of the day and part of the night until finally, with tears in her eyes, mother apologized and begged our forgiveness.

"I promise that for my sons and the love of God I will endure the cruelties of life in the Soviet Union."

She kept her vow.

# Chapter 8

# Overcoming the System

*"It is only the farmer who faithfully plants seeds in the Spring, who reaps a harvest in the Autumn."*

—B. C. Forbes

I was getting a little older and thought I'd like to earn some money of my own. My dear friend Vania introduced me to some men who lived in a nearby camp. They had horses and wagons which they used to haul dirt and supplies. Since I was interested in riding the horses, I volunteered to take them to pasture. I also knew the best places to graze, having tended the goats, so the men taught me how to tether the steeds so they could not run away during the night while they were feeding.

The "money" I received was a variety of things—sometimes real kopecks, sometimes tobacco, sometimes sunflower seeds; not much, but it was my very own. Some of the men couldn't pay me anything at all, but I would care for their horses just the same. I learned a valuable lesson that would serve me well for years to come: You do not always have to be paid immediately—people learn to depend on you and you will be rewarded later on.

Around this time I developed a crush on a pretty girl named Vala who lived in my neighborhood. It so happened that my mother bought me my first new shirt, a white one. I had always worn my brother's hand-me-downs, and I was so proud of my very own brand new shirt that I wanted Vala to see me wearing it; all I needed was a reason. I summoned up the courage to invite her to the movies where I could spend all my hard-earned money on lovely Vala.

What I didn't know was that Vala had another admirer, and this particular admirer happened to be sitting on the grass with a few friends, just outside the theater on the afternoon of our date. He was smoking a cigarette, waiting for the doors to open as Vala and I approached. When he saw the two of us his eyes flashed. He jumped up and grabbed me by the front of my shirt. When he did this, the flare of his cigarette burned a hole through my new shirt. He was four or five years my senior and I was afraid that he was getting ready to "headbutt" me, a popular method of fighting in those days where the top of one's head is bashed into the mouth and nose area of an opponent. The end result was generally a broken nose or some missing teeth for the recipient of the headbutt.

Impulsively, perhaps out of fear, I quickly wrapped my left arm around my attacker's neck and held on as tightly as I could. I was sure I would be killed if he got loose. I started hammering away for dear life with my right fist, landing about twenty good punches before I released him. He staggered back and fell to the ground. I looked down at him and saw the bloody evidence of the battle all over my new shirt. Apologetically I bid Vala farewell and ran home to have my new shirt cleaned and mended. Quite a memorable first date.

In the Fall of 1939 Anatole was drafted into the Red Army for a second time. Soon after in November the Soviet Forces invaded Finland in order to regain land lost through negotiations after World War I. But much to the surprise of the Russians, the miniscule Finnish military effectively fended off the much larger Russian Army until March, 1940. The Finns were defeated by sheer numbers. The U.S.S.R. then installed a communist government in the village of Terijoki, headed by Otto Kuusien.

When Anatole returned home from the battles, he told of how unprepared the Soviet Army was. The casualties were estimated at forty Russian soldiers lost for every one Finnish soldier killed. He told of the Finnish soldiers effective use of camouflage. They dressed all in white and came skiing down the snow covered hills at more than fifty miles per hour, machine guns blazing, to attack unsuspecting Soviet convoys. These attacks, together with buried land mines, sometimes resulted in the deaths of up to two hundred Soviet soldiers.

The poor showing of the Soviets in this tiny country may have convinced Hitler that he could quickly defeat the Soviets. Materials such as oil, manganese, chromium and grain were already flowing to Germany from Russia to bolster the Nazi war machine. Stalin's generosity was motivated by fear and he unwittingly helped Germany prepare for its next move. He even gave Hitler several hundred German communist refugees in Brest Litovsk. The NKVD (Secret Police) handed them over to the Gestapo and they were indiscriminately placed in concentration camps. Stalin was accommodating because he did not want democracy to flourish.

In our home during that winter, we continued to be as helpful to mother as possible. She gained some weight back and appeared to regain her bearings on life.

Vania was drafted into the Red Army and participated in the invasion of Poland. He was injured when a barrel fell from a truck and struck him. It earned him a hospital stay of a couple of months. When he was released from duty and returned home, he told mother how clean Poland was and how the Poles had a higher standard of living, apparent even in wartime. As proof he managed to bring home scarves and blankets that were far superior in quality to any of those produced in the U.S.S.R.

The trains of boxcars filled with Poles, Lithuanians, Estonians, Latvians, and Rumanians sojourning through Darnica station in 1940 became a daily occurrence. When the trains stopped briefly at the station and I could detect a boxcar carrying Poles I would exchange my rubles for Polish coins, if the guards allowed it.

In April the benevolence of Stalin spread to the Poles when he approved the massacre of 15,000 Polish officers held in Zakopane, occupied Poland, taken during the invasion of Poland. Stalin had never honored the rules set by the Geneva Convention, claiming it to be a capitalistic bourgeois convention. The brutal act against the Polish officers was well coordinated between the NKVD and the Gestapo and deemed "an action against Polish nationalism." While the massacre took place, Soviet and German officers frolicked about the former resort town in horse-drawn sleds.

Stalin continued his stalling and appeasing tactics with Hitler to give him time to better prepare his troops to avoid a repeat of the war in Finland. Paradoxically, purges of the military brass continued and many Red Army chiefs were executed or sent to rot uselessly in Soviet jails. On May 4 Stalin replaced war commissar Voroshilov, Feodor's uncle, with Timoshenko.

In Berlin, Hitler ended eight months of watching and waiting. On May 10 the Nazi forces undertook a blitzkrieg against Holland, Belgium, Luxembourg and France. The demise of France proved to be swift and by June 22 almost all of Europe was under Hitler's control.

With the spring came farming. As usual, collective farms were operated in a sluggish and disorganized manner. Villagers living on the fringes of Kiev worked hard, but only on their illegal plots of land. They seeded the rich, black Ukrainian soil with a variety of vegetables in the hopes of averting the hunger that had become an integral part of Russia's character.

Mother was no different. With shovel in hand she prepared her vegetable garden by planting radishes, potatoes, green onions and tomatoes. As she worked in the garden and was warmed by the spring sun, her focus was turned from her missing husband to the Supreme Mother—Nature. Zan and I assisted her as she gave her all to the soil, and soon to the little sprouts that began to protrude.

There was a new chicken farm nearby which became a good source of fertilizer and Zan and I made frequent quick trips there with our large basket. Although the farm was run by the government, the chicken excrement was made available to the public free of charge; if only the chickens had been as well. Unfortunately getting a chicken meant hours of waiting in line at the local government store and it cost a precious ruble as well.

Living conditions began to improve for our family when mother became a kiosk manager and opened a kiosk for dispensing chocolate and vanilla ice cream. Her kiosk was within walking distance of our apartment at the intersection of two of Kiev's unpaved streets. The government had built four wooden three-foot by five-foot whitewashed kiosks where a vendor was allowed to sell one type of item. Each kiosk

*The arrow points to the ice cream kiosk managed by Josephine*

had a door in back and a window on each of the four sides. Her ice cream was packed two canisters per wooden oval barrel. The barrels were located on the right side of the customer window as one faced out of the booth.

Across from her kiosk was one that sold warm beer. Kitty-corner, another sold baked goods. The kiosk manager beside her peddled carbonated water with five or six different flavors, including cherry and strawberry.. The soda manager was a plump, elderly lady who would encourage me to sift through the sand under the kiosks in search of lost kopecks. Every evening I did just that with a long, thin pole. I was rewarded, just as she had predicted, not only with coins but with bottle caps and other metal scraps which I used for barter.

When it came to changing the five-gallon cartons of ice cream stored in the wooden barrels, I was mother's helper. The two canisters per barrel were loaded with a lot of ice, salt and sawdust. Since the Soviets did not have ice making machines, the ice was harvested from local riverbeds in the winter. Ice production was under the strict supervision of a Commissar of Ice Production for the Soviet Union. Workers cut ice from the rivers in huge blocks which were then formed into pyramids at suitable locations. They then covered the pyramids with a layer of sawdust and a thick layer of straw for insulation. By doing this, the ice supply lasted throughout the summer.

Mother had to account for every scoop of ice cream sold—so many portions per canister, so much per portion. She had to forfeit many of her rubles to the government per day as an operation tax. Although the paper cups that held the ice cream gave her a slight advantage in weight, it was not enough. An ethical woman ordinarily, she was forced to use a kopeck on the scales in order to make enough rubles so that she could give the government their due and still have a few left over for us to survive on. Had she ever been caught using the additional kopeck weight, it would have meant jail for her.

Often at the intersection where the kiosks stood, an unkempt old man would appear, dressed in worn out, rumpled clothing, shouting the "truth" about the Communist Party. His rantings always attracted a large audience. The local militia men tolerated him because he was mentally retarded.

They even enjoyed him, so they continued to let him shout his piece.

On some occasions I would deliver a portion of ice cream to an old German lady who lived close by. My mother had known her for many years. She lived in apartment no larger than a small walk-in closet. There was not even room for a table; instead, she used a chair to serve as such. The Folk Deutch frau had no money with which to reward me for my delivery, so she substituted education for pay, teaching me the German language a few words at a time. She would teach me one day, then ask me what I remembered the following day. Slowly, I picked up many German words and phrases. I liked her very much and considered her an intellect.

There were many other changes that summer. Anatole and Hala married and moved to Kiev. Zan was drafted into Red service, and Henry moved out and now lived in Kiev. Henry was interested in photography and took courses in film-making. He took a summer job operating movies in a "kino" van that traveled from village to village. The Ukrainian and Russian villages he visited had no movie theaters, so he hung up a sheet on the side of the truck to serve as a screen. The movies were mainly Soviet propaganda showing things such as how happy life was on collective farms. He would occasionally return home bearing dried mushrooms and fruit.

The "worker's paradise" of Henry's films was far from reality. While the *Pravda* magnified communist progress and suppressed any sentiment to the contrary, young people had resorted to stealing and murder. Gangs ruled the avenues of Kiev after dusk. Armed with straight razors, they would slash leather watchbands and wrists to steal a watch, leaving the shocked victim rooted to the spot, dripping blood. Hooligans spread terror on Kiev's buses. The incidents were reported to members of the militia who completely ignored the majority of them. It was not a good time to be a child. Childhood was stolen from children, just as were the watches and other possessions of the innocent.

I was very jealous of Henry's roaming, so I took revenge by beating him in chess. Since the age of six I had spent hours practicing the game with boys of all ages, and I took a perverse delight in my victories over Henry.

Fun and games, however, were minimal in my life. The chess matches were a part of sibling rivalry at its innocent best. However, a deeper seed of jealousy was growing in me due to mother's apparent abundant love and favoritism of Zan. She spoke of him constantly. I felt that Anatole and Henry merited second place in her heart and I came in last. This weighed heavily upon me.

On August 20, 1940, while in exile in Mexico, Leon Trotsky was murdered with an ice pick according to Stalin's directives. Trotsky had previously been the war commissar but was expelled from the Red Party and banished from Russia for opposing Stalin's authoritarian rule and advocating worldwide revolution. Following his murder, Trotskyites in the Soviet Union were arrested on a grand scale. Soon the trains transporting Stalin's enemies to Siberia could not keep up with his purges—there were simply not enough trains. As a solution, many would-be workers were executed and buried in mass graves throughout the Soviet countryside.

Henry voluntarily joined the Red Army to serve as a cameraman. He sent notice to mother, asking that she and I come to the institute to say goodbye. Mother took the news badly that her son had joined ranks with the same people who had seized her husband. Nevertheless, she complied. By the time mother and I arrived at the institute, Henry was already gone.

He wrote to us for a while, but we were never to see him again.

# INVADERS

## The New Authority

# Chapter 9
# The German Storm

*"The only remedy, and one that might seem visionary, is the acquisition of greater living space—a quest that has in every age been the origin of the formation of states and of the migration of peoples."*

—Adolf Hitler

In spite of the Molotov-Ribbentrop Pact signed by Germany less than two years prior, German troops had been positioning themselves closer and closer to the Ukrainian border. Then early one morning a German bomber appeared directly over Kiev. Instead of dropping explosives, thousands of leaflets poured down from the blue sky, penned with German propaganda. The message inscribed was coherent and succinct: "Do not resist. We have come to liberate you from the Communist Government." The message went on to promise the Ukrainian people their own government, police force and army under German direction. The pamphlets were signed by Adolph Hitler.

The people were uncertain as to whether they could trust the Germans. Their only source of information was the *Pravda* which only contained news the communists wished to be read. They were, however, certainly weary of the murderous Stalin.

The eve of Operation Barbarosa, the German attack, was June 22, 1941. Hitler renounced the nonaggression pact and unleashed the full fury of the German troops and weapons upon the backward Soviet nation. A stunned Stalin announced over the radio, "Budiyet morda bita u Hitlera bandyta!" ("We will slap Hitler's face, who is a bandit!") Then he retreated into seclusion for a few days. Stalin had ignored reports from both Western and Soviet intelligence which stated that Hitler was preparing for a massive attack. The defeat of the U.S.S.R. would deal a hard blow to communism.

On July 3, Stalin addressed his citizens and attempted to revive and motivate the tired and depressed people to rally against the German invaders. Citizens were expected to fight to the death for the honor of Mother Russia and, to that end, being taken prisoner would be considered a crime and be judged an act of treason. He ordered the military to "fight the advancing German armies to the next to the last bullet. Commit suicide with the last bullet."

Bomb shelters were dug feverishly day and night as Kiev's population moved underground. The people of the city lived on constant alert for German bombers. Thousands moved into the Ural Mountains or north to Moscow. Horse drawn wagons crept along the sides of the roads, away from the shelling and urban death. Cars and tanks moved in the same direction on the left, not much faster. Above the roads flew the Luftwaffe, its planes spraying the river of people and vehicles with machine gun fire. Pandemonium reigned. Massacred women held dying children in their arms. Dead horses and burning vehicles made progress next to impossible.

The daily shelling of Kiev and the surrounding area usually began around 9:00 a.m., so people made certain they were in a shelter by that time. I was amazed by the accuracy of the barrage from the German artillery, not realizing that they used a spotter plane to direct the fire.

The constant pounding from the air raids was trying and unnerving; it caused the people to suffer greatly. One morning I hesitated just outside the shelter, dreading the prospect of having to spend another day within. I didn't realize how close it was to nine o'clock until a bursting shell knocked me to the ground. Then another shell with a terrifying, whistling sound exploded, killing a woman only inches from me. I stared at her for an instant, then dashed into the shelter and shook the dirt from my clothing. For the rest of the day I tried to forget the look on the dead woman's face. I haven't yet.

Another morning, mother and I were settling down in the shelter with Vania, Dasha and their two little girls. In the quiet of the shelter, Dasha tried to remember whether or not she had locked their stable door to keep the frightened cow from running away during the shelling. Since it was several minutes before the shelling was to begin, she decided to go and check the door.

"Dasha, no, there is not time," pleaded Vania.

"It is our only cow. Don't worry, I will be back in time." She quickly dashed out.

Dasha made it to the stable and had started back to the shelter when the shelling began, early. A piece of shrapnel from an exploding shell ripped her chest apart and she fell to the ground, dead.

That evening I watched Vania tenderly pick Dasha up and carry her home through the stench of the streets littered with dead horses and decaying corpses. I remembered how, only a few short years before, he had carried her to our kitchen from the tall grasses beyond the creek.

When the soldiers of the Red Army retreated, they chose to burn everything they were unable to mobilize, rather than leave behind anything that might be useful to the Germans. This left much of Kiev devastated. As the German army approached the city, Stalin ordered bridges, apartments, warehouses, factories, even hospitals to be blown up. Since there was no time to evacuate the citizens from these buildings, they were sacrificed as well.

The station in Darnica and trains there were filled with Soviet soldiers when they were blown apart—even a train of the wounded. I witnessed this and wept. I felt I was, at thirteen years of age, facing the prophesied Armageddon.

Looters took the opportunity to scavenge anything that had not been destroyed from the burned out shells of warehouses. Many of the looters, though, were just ordinary citizens who had been deprived of everyday amenities. I even ventured into one warehouse with a friend. In one dark corner of the garbage-strewn floor we found two barrels labeled SUNFLOWER OIL that had either gone unnoticed or were too burdensome to be whisked away during the chaotic raid on this particular warehouse. My friend and I simply rolled the barrels out and down the middle of the street, pretending we were playing a game so as not to attract attention.

When I arrived at home with my barrel of treasure, I buried it under the porch, covering it with dirt and sand to hide it well. I left just a small area uncovered where I made a puncture. Through this hole I inserted a small rubber hose so the oil could be siphoned out and used for cooking. Mother used it for potato pancakes. I gave some to the neighbors and sold some to others.

The morning after I found my liquid treasure, the artillery did not speak in its usual barrage. We all knew that it meant the German troops were very near. Midmorning a lone German soldier entered Darnica riding a bicycle. He stopped, laid it on the ground along with his weapon, and opened up a sandwich. While he ate, we watched through crevices to see what his next move would be. He looked around and continued to eat his sandwich. Then, one by one, Red Army soldiers emerged from their hiding places and walked toward the lunching German. He stopped eating and sat frozen, apparently not knowing what to expect. When the soldiers reached him they simply laid their weapons on the ground and put their hands in the air. More Red Army soldiers came, now in groups, to surrender to this single German soldier. He stood, herded them together, and lead the group of at least two hundred out of the village. It was quite a sight to behold.

Soon more German soldiers entered Darnica on bicycles to check out the streets. More and more Red Army soldiers surrendered themselves to these Germans.

I noticed one soldier having trouble with his bike. "Ferflukte bicycle kaput!" he cursed while he shook it. He gave it a final kick and left it under a tree and walked off. I knew it was forbidden to take anything belonging to the military, but my desire for a bicycle was overwhelming. It overrode the thought of possible consequences. I casually strolled down the street toward the tree by the bicycle. I leaned against the tree for a bit, then sat down on the grass and waited. As the dusk drew into Darnica and I felt no one was paying attention, I casually picked up the two-wheeled vehicle and walked it home where I stashed it under the porch. There was now room under the porch for my new treasure since the goats had been housebroken and were now kept in the kitchen so they wouldn't be stolen.

The following morning the roaring of the German tanks entering Darnica served as an alarm clock for those who were able sleep. Mother and I watched as many of the women of the village ran from their houses to greet the soldiers with flowers and food. "The Germans are here! We are liberated from Stalin!" was their cry.

German troops met no resistance in Darnica or Kiev. I personally admired the dapper soldiers with their pressed uniforms and shiny tanks. The Soviets could never resist such well-equipped and orderly German armies, I thought.

# Chapter 10

# Under German Tyranny

*"If we lose this war, God help us."*

—*Reich Marshal Hermann Goring*

It had only been a short while since we welcomed the Germans with flowers. Now, the invaders held 660,000 Soviet prisoners of war. Mass executions were an everyday occurrence. We had become victims of the same brutality we'd endured under Stalin—only the uniforms had changed.

Outwardly, the civilian population cooperated with German authorities. German commanders immediately put the POWs to work rebuilding railroad lines and constructing barracks. Darnica's railroad station was rebuilt easily in three days because the Germans supplied the POWs with prefabricated components. Repairing the tracks was not as simple. Dynamite had been discharged in the roadbed every twenty feet.

Even though life under Nazi rule was becoming increasingly intolerable, I could not help but favorably compare the efficiency of the German army to the lack of the same in the ill-equipped, neglected Soviet soldiers.

The loss of Kiev infuriated Stalin. He ordered the execution of four commissars for "anti-Soviet activities." This was the beginning of his purging. Not satisfied, on August 16, 1941 he signed order #270 which stated that "officers and political workers captured by Germans will be treated as malicious deserters. Their families will be subject to arrest. Families of any captured soldiers will be deprived of state assistance." Since all food was rationed by the government this meant, in essence, that the families of POWs would starve to death.

Even Stalin's son, Yakov Dzhugashvili, was not exempt. When he fell into German hands, Hitler offered to exchange him for a captured German general. Stalin refused. He considered Yakov a traitor for having been captured alive. Yakov threw himself onto the electrified fence of the POW camp and was then shot and killed by a guard. Stalin's own wife, Yulia, was arrested and imprisoned for two years.

Finland, Romania, and Hungary joined the Germans. After the Japanese bombing of Pearl Harbor the United States entered the war. Winston Churchill offered Stalin England's help to fight off Hitler.

The construction camp, my boyhood home, was now occupied by the Germans. A new kitchen had been constructed by the water well and was now manned by Soviet POWs. I frequently walked the main thoroughfare which passed between two fenced-off sections of the camp. It was the only route between my house and the village.

*A slaughtered cow confiscated by Germans soldiers as they "lived off the land."*

One day I stood watching a POW debone some pork. I was only about thirty feet away but out of sight. The POW decided to suck the marrow from a large bone before discarding it,

64

thinking no one was watching. It was forbidden to taste anything being prepared for the "super race."

Unfortunately, a gestapo guard saw what he had done. He called over another guard and they ordered the man to dig his own grave.

"Now lay in your grave," one guard would order. "Get back out," ordered the other. "Take off your boots." "Get back in the grave." "Get out again." They continued this for about an hour until they weren't amused anymore. Then the first guard shot the man in the head. Another POW who was ordered to bury him asked the guard if he could keep the dead man's boots. He was probably lucky all he got was a "no."

A train loaded with food supplies for the German soldiers sat on a track a few miles from the Darnica depot. It was guarded by a Ukrainian soldier in German uniform. My friends and I had watched this guard march back and forth many times. We counted how many minutes it took him to get from one end of the train to the other, and we came up with a plan: once the guard had passed a boxcar near to us, we would break into it.

The guard passed on schedule and we ran up to the door, broke the seal, and quickly slipped inside. The car was loaded with eggs. Unfortunately, as the guard passed on his return, he noticed the broken seal and slid the door open. We froze. He pointed raised his gun and pointed it at us. "Leave at once or I will shoot!"

It was common knowledge that the Ukrainians were only given one round of ammunition—the Germans didn't trust them.

"Go ahead and shoot one of us. Then the rest of us will kill you." After a moment, the guard lowered his weapon and marched to the other end of the train.

That same day mother had taken one of father's jackets and ventured through the countryside attempting to barter it for food. She eventually found a farmer who gave her six eggs for it.

I was already home when mother arrived. She told me how pleased she was that she would be able to prepare eggs for us and proudly displayed the eggs. I could not help myself and laughed out loud. She looked very perplexed. I went to the bed and pulled off the blanket that covered the entire crate of eggs I brought from the train. The details of their procurement remained my secret, though.

Anatole had "obtained" an old Russian truck. He had actually put it together with body and engine parts he scavenged from abandoned trucks scattered throughout the countryside. The Germans gave him a permit to drive it as long as he would deliver coal for them three days a week for no pay. He agreed, and was able to work the other four days for himself.

When Anatole had come for a visit, I told him that I had taken a discarded German bicycle but I didn't fix it for fear of being found out. Big brother came to my rescue. He took the bicycle apart and obliterated anything that would link it to its Czechoslovakian origin. After we repainted the entire bike, the original problem which had caused the soldier to abandon it still remained: two ball bearings were missing from the back wheel. At this point I called up a little of my own ingenuity and cut some razor blades into small pieces to use for spacers. Common lard replaced the ball bearing grease, and viola!—I was at last a man with transportation.

Each day I would tend the goats and horses as quickly as possible so I could be free to ride around for a few hours. I observed the daily actions of the Germans, especially the trains going in and out of Darnica's yards, wondering still if one day my father might return on one of them. I learned to salute and say "Heil Hitler!" as I approached German officers. Sure enough, they smiled and returned the salute.

Romanian and Italian soldiers were now entering Kiev to join the Germans in their battle with the Soviet Army. The Romanians would trade their rations for onions as protection against scurvy. They were good fighters as well. The

Italians wore hats decorated with a fancy plume and sabers on their belts. Their interests tended more toward wine and women. In fact, many times the Italians would grab and mishandle women, using their superior position as "conquerors" to their advantage. Their actions dismayed the German officers, sometimes to the point of placing them in detention. If detainees were repeat offenders, it was not unheard of for one of them to be shot.

Mother continued carrying her LUKOWSKI sign, walking along the barbed wire fences of the POW camps in the area hoping for word of Henry or her pet, Zan. As each day passed with no news, she slipped further and further into depression. She became angry with the world and often took it out on me. Her attitude toward me grew to be so negative that I decided to go to live with Anatole and Hala in Kiev.

Going into the city was no longer a simple matter. The Germans had rebuilt only one bridge and, because of the fear of sabotage, it was used strictly for military purposes or by those with special permission. A dusk to dawn curfew had been put into effect which meant no walking in the streets at night.

I desperately wanted to go to my brother, so I broke the curfew and left home in the evening. As I approached the snow covered, frozen Dniepier River, I could see the Nazis patrolling the bridge and the streets of Kiev. About 150 soldiers were on watch at the bridge twenty-four hours a day.

I crawled into some bushes by the edge of the snow covered river and was startled by an elderly man hiding there. He also hoped to cross the one-third mile wide frozen void and reach the city. Together we watched the searchlight on the bridge.

"You see?" he whispered to me. " It passes completely over the river every fifty seconds. This will give us forty seconds to run before we must drop down into the snow for cover."

I nodded in agreement.

We felt comfortable with our plan. The man began counting the seconds. When the time was right, he headed out of the brush.

"Don't follow me right away. Wait a bit." Then he was gone.

I did as he instructed, following about sixty feet behind him. We had reached the midpoint of the river and it suddenly became apparent to me that he had miscalculated. I dropped down. He was still running when the searchlight picked him up. There was a short burst of gunfire and the man fell.

I lay where I was, breathing heavily. I looked toward the man but he did not make the slightest motion. I was certain he was dead. When the searchlight passed I took off again, hitting the snow before it swept over me on the way back. I continued this routine—counting, running, dropping down—until I reached the safety of the bushes on the other side. I breathed a sigh of relief. I had made it. Now just seven blocks remained to Anatole's apartment.

It took quite some time to travel those seven blocks. I had to creep along buildings and duck into doorways, but I finally reached their door. Hala opened it and gasped when she saw my frozen condition. She quickly pulled me inside and tried to take off my shoes, but she couldn't; my feet had swollen so much from the cold that she had to cut the shoes to remove them. My feet were now as white as the snow that had frozen them.

Hala took a pan outside and filled it with snow. She brought it to me and had me put my feet into it and then spent the next several hours massaging them vigorously. I never realized what frostbite entailed—the pain that came with the return of my circulation proved excruciating. Anatole came home in the wee hours of the morning after hauling some goods for the Germans and found me in bad shape. We soon retired for the night. The apartment contained only a single kerosene burner for cooking as well as heating. Since the supply of kerosene was unstable, everyone conserved when they could. We huddled together in one bed for the warmth necessary to survive the winter night.

Before drifting off to sleep, I thought about the kind man who had tried to lead me safely across the river. I could see his motionless form, dark against the snow. I was very sorry to have lost him.

The next few days were miserable for me as I dealt with the stinging in my feet and the separation from my mother, until one day there was a knock at the door. It was Mother. She had come to visit Hala. Being an older woman crossing the bridge before curfew, she had an easier time getting approval for passage. I was uncomfortable with her there and things were cool between us. While she was preparing to leave at the end of her visit, she suggested that I return home for a bath since Anatole's apartment had no tub and was not warm enough anyway. This broke the ice between us and I went with her back to Darnica.

The winter food crisis worsened. Cats and dogs disappeared from the streets of Kiev and the surrounding areas. Cannibalism once again returned to the masses. The bread rationed to civilians was made from ground acorns, sawdust and a bit of flour. It tasted like wallpaper paste. Mother had killed the goats for food because of the heavy tax imposed on livestock by the Germans. Rubles were now worthless except to use for cigarette rolling paper. The black market grew and became the best source for obtaining food.

Vania and I took to wandering the frozen countryside looking for matches, salt or cigarettes to trade for food. Often we were able to trade homemade vodka to German and Italian soldiers for food. At one point in our journey Vania spotted a mound on the flat landscape and climbed it to have a better look around for shelter. The mound turned out to be the three frozen bodies of people who had stopped on their sled for a rest and had frozen to death. We kept walking.

On another trip out, I was given shelter by a farm family who let me share a bed built into the wall of their wood burning fireplace. In the morning light when I returned from running barefoot to the outhouse in the terrible cold, I noticed that the feet of the family members were all black. I guessed they had not bathed all winter.

When I returned home I told mother about the overnight. We discovered I had picked up lice. She readied a tub of hot water for me on the porch while I undressed. As I bathed and deloused in the warm water, she took my clothes inside to boil for their own delousing.

One of the warehouses where I once played in the German-occupied construction camp was filled with grain. It so happened that many years before I had made a "secret gate" in the surrounding fence by removing the bottom nails of some of the fence boards, never realizing that it would prove useful to me later in life. I devised a plan to get some of that grain.

I picked an interested friend and the two of us, empty sacks in hand, stole into the yard through the secret gate. The warehouse and all the other buildings had been constructed on stilts because of the spring floods. We crawled under the grain warehouse and stuck a knife up through a space in the wooden plank flooring into one of the sacks of grain. The golden sustenance poured down to us and we quickly filled our bags.

All the while Mother and I continued our search for word of Henry and Zan with the LUKOWSKI sign Henry had prepared for father. The Germans had thousands of prisoners of war, most kept behind barbed wire without food or water.

Some were used as oxen and made to pull carts filled with stone, wood or sand. We heard that a thousand died per day.

I once saw one of these captives move away from his cart, gesturing to the guard that he must relieve himself by the roadside. The guard shot him.

When the men were marched somewhere, it was ten abreast. If it was necessary to cross the bridge, some would risk being shot jumping into the river; and they were, often before hitting the water or shortly thereafter. Countless bodies floated in the river.

One day while I busied myself raking the backyard, I was startled to hear, "How are you, Turek?" I turned to see an unshaven man in a shaggy Russian uniform. I stared at him a bit before I recognized his face. It was Wilhelm, the son of the Folks Deutsche lady who taught me German in return for ice cream deliveries. He had served in the Red Army during the Invasion of Poland. He told me that he had received heavy wounds and was later captured by the Germans. He never completely recovered, so the Germans released him from the POW camp; he was returning home for the first time.

I learned from him that Zan had been in his platoon and that he was fine.

"Please, let my mother know that I am coming home. I do not want the shock of seeing me to be too much for her," he said.

Fortunately, Wilhelm's brother Ludwig was at home when I went to the house. I asked him to come with me. He was overjoyed when he saw Wilhelm, and excitedly went to tell his mother the good news. A wonderful, happy reunion followed. Wilhelm told them that he had walked 600 miles to get home, living off the land. His desire to be with his family had kept him alive.

I ran home to tell mother the news about Zan. She said that she had always known that Zan would survive the war but that Henry would perish. She had gone to several psychics and they all said the same thing.

Wilhelm would die soon after of complications from his wounds, but at least it was in the arms of his beloved.

In the Spring of 1943 the SS changed their attitude towards deserters. Instead of shooting them, they now preferred to torture them. Once as I was walking with a friend near the old construction camp, we noticed four human heads on the ground close to the fence. We stopped to look at them and saw the eyes in the heads blink. Then the heads moved slightly. I later learned from Vania that this was the punishment for deserters who were caught. After a couple days in the ground they were forced to join an SS "suicide outfit." This was their second chance. Most all would soon die in action.

Stalin's morale began to improve when the United States' Lend Lease program went into effect. Russia received 50 million dollars worth of war equipment which enabled him to keep Port Murmansk open.

Whole grain was more accessible to us than flour. Since the local mills were charging 20% of the grain for milling it, Vania and I decided to build our own mill. We punched about a thousand holes in a piece of sheet metal with a nail and mounted it around a slightly tapered wooden cylinder, sharp edges out. Vania drilled a hole in the center of the cylinder for an axle and a crank. The whole mechanism was then inserted into a tight-fitting length of pipe with a flange. Our mill served us well for as long as we needed it.

Hitler had sent notices out to all the Jewish people in Kiev that they were to be repatriated to Israel. He designated an area near Kiev called Baby Yar for them to assemble with whatever goods they wished to bring for their journey to their new land. Some Jewish people brought furniture, even pianos. Many Ukrainians were hired to help carry these goods to Baby Yar.

Not one person who entered there survived. After they were assembled, the Germans shot them—90,000 Jews and 37,000 Ukrainians, men, women and children—all dead.

Shortly thereafter, mother and I came upon a girl in her late teens sitting on a tree stump in the forest, crying.

"You must be a Jew from Kiev," mother said.

The girl didn't deny it, but only sobbed more. She was very pitiful.

"If you are Jewish, you are in grave danger. Wait here," mother told her. She then hurried to Vania's house. He still had Dasha's identification papers and gave them to mother for the girl. She returned and gave her the papers and directed her to a village far away from Kiev. With the papers and a stroke of luck, perhaps she survived.

I continued to struggle for survival in my own way, too. When we were running low on grain, I would go back to the old construction camp and get some from below the planks of the warehouse floor. I also discovered that the Germans would trade food for certain metals. The exchange rate for brass and lead was an equal weight in grain. I busied myself collecting lead because it was the heaviest and I could get it easily from abandoned artillery shells left in the nearby wetland. I dismantled anti-aircraft shells, emptied and burned the explosive, and recovered the lead projectiles. This was all done without mother's knowledge. She thought I was just seeking some adventure in the country. I didn't want her to worry.

For a long time mother had wanted to leave the Soviet Union for Poland where her brothers and sisters lived in Krasnovice and Ostrovo. She felt that she and I would have a better chance of surviving there. She had wanted Anatole and his family to come also. Although Anatole liked the idea very much, he realized that with Vladimir, the new addition to his family, the trip would be impossible for them.

The Germans gave us permission to board a train heading West. For the two days before we were to leave, we disposed of most of our possessions. Some things went to Anatole and Vania and some were sold on the black market. Mother asked Vania to give food to her missing sons should they survive the war and return.

Just before we left for Darnica station I saw Vala, the girl I had almost taken to a movie. She kissed me goodbye. We would never see each other again.

Vania, Anatole, Hala and a few other friends gathered at the station to see us off. We boarded after some tearful goodbyes and watched them waving to us as the train pulled out and headed west. Mother broke down and strained against the window to see the diminishing figure of Anatole until she could no longer make him out. It was September 20, 1943.

The front of the locomotive pulling our train was decorated with swastika flags. The first two cars were gondolas filled with sand, and behind these were many cars packed with people like ourselves, people fleeing west. The last three cars were first class cars reserved for German soldiers and these, naturally, were the safest in case someone had mined the tracks or tried to blow up the train.

After years of fruitless struggle in the "workers paradise" of the Soviet Union, mother was now hopeful for a better future for the two of us. She was fifty-one and I would soon turn fifteen. She knew that her family in Poland would assist us. In her heart she realized that she must take this, her first opportunity, and leave the Soviets. If it were not for the permission of the Germans, she and I would never have been able to leave Kiev.

We began to relax after a few hours of riding. We sat silently, staring out the window, watching the countryside roll past. I reminisced about the life I was leaving behind and I'm sure mother was doing the same.

The train came to an abrupt halt. In the distance we could see a burning village. Several flatbed trucks loaded with women and children approached the train. It was a common practice that, when a single man fighting in the underground was given refuge within the perimeter of a village, all the men of the village were murdered and the village itself was burned. The women and children were then shipped to Germany to work in forced labor camps. But why were the trucks heading to our train? There was almost dead silence as all of us in the car held our breath.

German soldiers surrounded the train and ordered it to be evacuated immediately. We gathered our things and stepped out. There was a freight train sitting on the next track where all the passengers were being herded by the Germans.

Mother's renewed sense of hope disappeared and was replaced by anxiety when she saw the people from the trucks as well being loaded into the freight cars.

"Please, we here are not partisans. We are citizens traveling to Poland. We have permission," mother pled to a German officer. He ignored her.

The car we were forced into was a typical human cargo boxcar—a small opening in the top for air, and a pile of straw in the center to serve as a toilet. Mother and I huddled together, knowing now that we were not going to Poland but to Germany to help sustain Hitler's monstrous war machine.

There were many delays along the way—long waits on rail sidings as trains with men and supplies heading east from Germany to supplement the Nazi troops were given priority.

The northwesterly, six-hundred-mile trip took eight days, with occasional stops to hand out buckets of water to the passengers and to replace the soiled straw. Compassionate guards would sometimes open the doors to let fresh air fill the cars because stops could last for hours.

Mother had cleverly placed some food and small bottles of homemade vodka in her basket hoping that, if opportunities presented themselves, she would be able to barter the vodka for rations from German soldiers. One guard replied "ja vol" to her request and gave her a round ball of swiss cheese. She kept both of us fed in this manner.

Many of the other passengers from Kiev were not as well prepared because a trip to Poland, under normal conditions, would not take so long. The women and children from the burned village were not prepared at all, so on two of the stops the guards brought bread which they passed out to their "human cattle."

The train continued slowly winding toward Deutschland. Mother peeked through the door as we passed a station and saw "Opol" on the sign. It was a Polish town she had known as a girl. Now it was annexed to Germany. She traveled through her homeland, our original destination, without ever touching a toe to its familiar soil.

# Chapter 11

# Incarceration in Germany

*"Custody of prisoners for security or preventive reasons is no longer the primary consideration. Emphasis has now shifted to the economic side."*

*—from a letter by Oswald Pohl to Reichsfuhrer SS Heinrich Himmler*

"All men to the left! All women to the right!" The train had finally come to rest at a place called Luneburg. The guards hurried us out of the cars and into an immense room, where we were ordered to strip down and put all of our clothing in baskets. I tried to see around the men in line in front of me. This is it, I thought. They're going to kill us in the next room.

I stepped through the door. It was a shower room with warm water and soap that felt like clay. The tension left me as I washed and felt clean for the first time since we had boarded the boxcar a week ago. After we were finished in the showers we were dusted with DDT from long metal cylinders to kill hair and body lice and protect us from certain diseases. Our clothes were put through a heat treatment to kill any remaining lice. Each person then had a picture taken for identification cards and given an "OST" label which signified the person as being from the East.

As terrible as it was to be a prisoner, once again I could not help but marvel at the efficiency of the Germans. If this processing of people was in the Soviet Union it would

*Arthur's I.D. card photo*

have taken days, not hours, and the showers would have run out of hot water.

Following the processing, mother and I and some other prisoners were put on a train for a short ride to Beckdorf—a labor camp that would become our home for almost three years. Beckdorf was established for the purpose of maintaining the railroad line from Hollenstat to Hamburg. It proved to be good fortune for all forty-four of us sent there because it was probably the smallest in Germany. Some camps housed thousands of prisoners and the chances of survival were not as good.

Beckdorf was a one-barrack camp. The barrack contained five rooms, the largest of which held forty-four bunk beds, each with a straw-filled mattress. A pot-belly stove stood in the center of the room to provide warmth. There was a small room with two sinks and a bathtub. The tub was essentially useless though, since there was no hot water. At the far end was a doorway to a small corridor that led to a mess hall filled with wooden tables and benches. On the other side of the mess hall was a kitchen and, just off the kitchen, sleeping quarters for ten guards. Outside near the barbed wired fence were the separate latrines for men and women. Only the camp manager and the elderly cook resided outside the camp; everyone else in Beckdorf was housed under one roof.

By the time we got settled, mother and I were much too exhausted from the train ride and processing to be concerned about anything but getting some rest. I fell asleep on a top bunk, with mother on the bunk below.

The next morning at 6:00 a.m. a harsh voice bellowed, "Auf steigen, bitte!" It meant we had to go outside to the yard to be counted and get a job assignment. The camp manager, a man in his fifties wearing a black SS uniform, marched out in front of the group. He was followed by the camp guards, all of whom were apparently past sixty. "SS" stood for "Schutzstaffel" which literally translated means "defense

*Josephine's I.D. card photo*

squadron." SS men policed the entire German army, protected Hitler, controlled the Gestapo—they were the most fanatical group in the Nazi Party.

Beside the camp manager stood an interpreter with an "OST" label sewn on his shirt. It was his duty to translate the orders of the camp manager. We were informed that a work week was six days long, with Sundays off. Disobeying the guards meant a trip to a concentration camp.

*Art standing amid the remains of Camp Beckdorf.*

We began our march out of the camp along the railroad line which lay just outside. Every mile or so one group would be separated out to begin work while the rest continued on. Mother and I were in a group that maintained the Eisen Ban, the rail line that stretched from Bremerhaven, almost to Hamburg.

It didn't take long for us to learn what backbreaking work maintaining railroad beds actually was. Men and women alike shoveled and spread the heavy stone—more than twenty metric tons of it in a day. Once we had to unload the stone from the wagons as well as shovel and spread it.

The days wore on. I felt tired and weak most of the time, but mother could hardly move. Her spirits sank and she increasingly withdrew.

Camp food fell below the daily requirement for maintaining health. Every evening we received a bowl of watery soup. We considered ourselves fortunate indeed if ours contained a bit of potato. Accompanying the soup was a single slice of bread with a patch of margarine. Mother and I drank our soup and saved the bread for morning. After several months of this diet, people in the camp were just skin over bones with hollow eyes devoid of shine.

Mother constantly fretted about me being starved and used as a slave. It was deplorable to her. One day she noticed one of the younger women leaving the kitchen with a bulge under her blouse. Immediately suspicious, mother hurried over to the woman.

"What have you got?" she asked, and began tugging on the front of the woman's shirt. Several slices of bread fell to the floor.

"Thief! You are stealing food from the rest of us!" mother screamed. "From my son—." She was cut off in midsentence by the bellowing of the camp manager, calling her into the kitchen. When she entered he began beating her on the face and shoulders, blackening her eyes and splitting her lips. All of us in the camp now knew for sure that the woman was exchanging sexual favors for food.

Sometimes the Beckdorf crews would work down the line past a POW camp. Our crew moved close to one with American and British prisoners. They had apparently received packages from the Red Cross and, out of pity, tossed bars of chocolate and other treats to us through the fence.

On Sundays, especially during the summer, farmers would come to our camp to ask for help picking fruit or harvesting some other crop. Everyone volunteered for this extra work because we could pick up extra food and bring it back to camp as a reward.

The winter of 1943-1944 was very hard. Shoes began wearing out. As they did, the guards replaced them with canvas-topped wooden-soled shoes. If we could find newspaper or burlap sacks, we would stuff them inside our shoes or jackets for extra warmth.

Mother and I had endured our first winter in the camp, and the following spring and summer, but with the fall mother decided she would not survive the next winter. In spite of my pleading and crying, she decided to wage a hunger strike. I knew no woman her age in her weakened condition could continue to perform such hard labor under such adverse conditions and survive. She would drink only a little water and refused to eat the meager portions of food.

One of the guards noticed that mother wasn't eating and called the camp manager. He and the guard came to me, questioning me about my mother's behavior. I told them that she said she would rather starve than go on living under these circumstances.

The following morning mother and I were detained from our work crew. We sat alone in the mess hall, waiting for members of the gestapo to arrive. It was a dreadful wait. I just knew we were going to get a one-way ride to a concentration camp. The men from the gestapo arrived. They spoke with me and found my German adequate for the occasion. One of them typed up a report as I answered questions. My interrogation finished abruptly and they left.

That evening the camp manager came to me and told me they were going to place mother on a farm about five miles away. It seemed that in her defiance, mother actually did herself a favor. On the farm she would neither have to work as hard nor starve to death.

One of the guards asked me if I would consider entering into the German ranks as a soldier.

"You have blond hair and blue eyes. You could pass for German. Your mother would be taken care of an you would be considered a member of the of the Arian race, the supreme race."

I declined his offer. As much as I admired their efficiency, I could not tolerate their heavy-handed treatment of people. Donning a German uniform was never even a serious consideration of mine.

A short time after mother left I was given a different job: looking after railroad telegraph lines. I received my training from an elderly German man named Fritz. He took a liking to me and shared the contents of his lunch pail with me many times. He told me I was a quick learner, and I appreciated not having to slave on the rail beds. After a while I was able to take the train to the main station where I would meet Fritz and receive my instructions for the day.

During my train rides to and from the main station, I was met with a variety of reactions from the Deutsche people. Some passengers would move away—all the way to another car. As laborers at the camp, we received only a minute piece of soap each month, which lasted only a few days. There was nothing extra for detergent for clothes. I was embarrassed by my appearance and odor.

One older woman did not move away from me. When she got up to leave she gestured to me to be silent and she put something in my bag. This generous lady had slipped me a pound of butter.

Another day on the ride a lovely girl was staring at me, so I winked at her. At the end of the day when I returned to the station from my work assignment, a German policeman came up. He grabbed me by the front of my shirt.

"Who do you think you are?" he said, then slapped me. "What right do you have being familiar with a fraulein?" He slapped me some more. Fritz saw what was happening and hurried over. He worked his way between the two of us and pushed the officer back.

"Stop! This fellow is my best worker. You leave him alone or I will take you on myself!" The policeman muttered something and left.

"Arthur, I think it would be best if, from now on, you just watched the scenery outside the train," Fritz said as he gave me a wink.

Mother's living conditions had improved greatly on the farm. Whenever I was able, I would slip out of the camp at night and jog along the railroad ties to her farm. We would enjoy a visit together and whatever food she managed to salvage for me. On one of my return trips to the camp I slipped while I was climbing the barbed wire fence, cutting my hands scarring me for life. The camp manager saw my cut hands and discovered I had been slipping out at night. He threatened me with a trip to a concentration camp if it happened again.

The next day when I met Fritz I told him what had happened and that I was forbidden to see my mother again. He decided to help me out. At the end of the work day when I checked out at the main station, Fritz would put me to work raking the yard, sweeping the station or picking fruit from the trees in the small orchard. He would then call me in and pretend to apologize to me for making me miss the last train to Beckdorf. He said he was busy and just let the time slip away.

He'd then phone the camp manager.

"Art is not deserting. I kept him working too long at the station. It was my fault. You will see him tomorrow." He'd hang up and turn to me. "Okay, Art. Go visit your mother."

The farm where mother worked was run by a woman; her husband and sons were in the German army, fighting the war. She was by no means the picture of kindness regarding my mother. She made her eat in the barn where her sleeping room was. When one of her sons was home from the Soviet front on furlough and saw how Mother was treated, he cautioned his mother. "You had better let her eat at the table with everyone else. Germany is going to lose this war."

From that point on, mother was allowed to eat with the others in the kitchen.

One afternoon I was riding a rail car to work. I sat on the floor with my feet dangling outside, as most of the workers did, when my left heel got caught between two converging rails. My foot was twisted almost completely around and I was in agony. A few laborers carried me back to camp where I lay suffering all through the night. By daylight my foot was quite swollen and the camp manager decided that I should see a doctor. He sent a guard to escort me. The guard rode his bicycle beside me while I hobbled the two mile distance on a tree branch. The doctor's office was on the second floor of a building and I had to crawl up on my hands and knees, in terrible pain. The doctor took a quick look at my foot and knew I had suffered a dislocation. He tied me in a straight-backed chair—so I could not fall off and injure myself further, he said. Then he closed all the windows and the door before he explained that he was not allowed to give me any anesthesia; it was for German soldiers only. But he said I could scream as much as I wanted to. He grabbed my foot and gave it a quick jerk. I screamed as though my foot had been ripped off. It was over in a couple of seconds. I hobbled back to camp on my tree branch with the guard along side. The swelling disappeared in three days. The memory didn't.

It wasn't long after the foot incident when Fritz told me that he was leaving to serve in the German army and that I would be in charge of two assistants. I was just seventeen and a boss. It was an empowering rite of passage of sorts.

Air raids began striking Hamburg, a strategic port city not far from the camp. More and more Allied bombers flew over; fewer and fewer German ones.

Several POW camps nearby were sources of news as we passed. "It'll be over soon!" the prisoners called. Some were Yugoslavian and most generous. They passed us whatever food they had—sometimes even their last piece of bread. I'm sure with our dirty, ragged, malnourished appearance they thought we were worse off than they were.

The weeks of fighting in Stalingrad were a turning point in the war. The Red Army managed to hold on to its position, but sacrificed four million soldiers doing so. The Germans lost over one million. I would later find out that Zan had fought there and was wounded. Several thousand Soviet soldiers, including those in Zan's company, had gotten trapped near Mamai Hill by the troops of Field Marshal Paulus while they were attempting to reinforce the soldiers trying to regain control of Stalingrad. Under the command of General Vasily Chuikov, they crossed the Volga River in small boats. He organized a lifeline of ferries and broke his men up into small guerrilla-like fighting units. For months during daylight hours they defended the buildings in the city. By night they vanished and reappeared in new positions. The counter-offensive of Generals Zukow and Winter encircled Paulus, and the field marshal surrendered on January 31, 1943. The Reds took more than 90,000 prisoners, handing a major defeat to the Fuhrer.

My crew and I busied ourselves with telegraph line maintenance. One day, while high up on a pole, I spied two

British Mosquito planes coming towards me. I knew that because of their speed and distance the pilots could not tell if we were Germans or not. I slid down the pole in record time, leaving some skin behind and jumped into a nearby ditch not far from my crew members. I could hear the machine gun bullets riddling the ground close by. None of us were hit.

Another day while I was up on a pole I heard some gleeful singing coming from far down the tracks. I squinted and in the distance I could see a man walking on the railroad ties, staggering from rail to rail. I climbed down and could then hear the words, "Volga, volga mac radnaya." The man's voice thundered. He was dressed in a filthy Red Army uniform and held a bottle in one hand.

"Tovarish, Hermaniec kaput, have a drink! It is good vodka! Nazdrovie!" he said as he came up to me.

He took a drink then handed the bottle to me. I did likewise. Almost instantly my eyes grew wide and my breathing stopped. I dropped the bottle and it shattered on the rail. The Russian had gotten a bottle of methyl alcohol from a nearby airport; the Germans used it for antifreeze. He thought it was good—*vsio ravno*.

I threw up all the way back to camp. There, a woman who was too old to work anywhere else and had been given the job of cleaning up at the camp, saw me arrive and noticed my poor state.

"Synku, what did you eat or drink?" she asked.

I told her my story and she gave me water to drink, then left. In a few minutes she returned with a bottle full of milk.

"You poisoned yourself with wood alcohol," she explained. "You must drink all that milk." I did and vomited into a bucket. For three days nothing would stay in my stomach. I was fortunate I didn't die, though.

As the bombing of Hamburg increased, those of us in the camp had a tremendous amount of work to do. Often the rail lines were blown apart as Hamburg was being destroyed.

The airports were obliterated and as a result, highways became runways and forests, airplane hangars.

My crew and I no longer reported back to camp. We slept near the main station to be quickly sent to wherever we were needed most. We three were given the same rations as the German soldiers but, of course, worked much longer hours.

On more than one night I could have read a newspaper by the light of the violent bombing of Hamburg. A gas shortage forced the Germans to use wood burning generators. Some military vehicles had to be pushed by hand. Laborers wandered the city streets with buckets and dippers trying to salvage oil floating on puddles in bomb craters.

The brutality of the Germans grew with the reality of defeat. Hitler ordered that all factories and industries be destroyed. The soldiers of the meticulous, efficient, youthful army that had invaded my hometown were now retreating in their own land—as dirty, war-weary old men. I looked into the sky. It was covered with Allied bombers from horizon to horizon, all heading toward Berlin. The thousands of prisoners in the concentration and labor camps rejoiced. They knew the end of their domination by the "Master Race" was near.

The camp manager and the guards all disappeared. None of us knew exactly what to do. I surely wasn't going to sit around the camp—I had been confined too long. I ran out and climbed a nearby hill and there I could see Allied tanks approaching the town.

# Chapter 12
# Liberation

*"In the depth of winter, I finally learned that within me there lay an invincible summer."*

—*Albert Camus*

From my hilltop vantage point I watched as a group of three tanks moved closer to the town. One pulled away from the group, while the other two stayed back to cover it. Suddenly the forward tank was struck by gunfire and withdrew back to the other two tanks. Come on, come on, I thought impatiently. I'd waited through too many black days. I didn't want to see this gray day with its glimmer of hope turn into just another black one.

In a few seconds I understood why the tank had retreated when I saw six British Spitfires buzz the German holdout position and riddle it with bullets. Within two hours all the remaining pockets of resistance on the edge of the town had been cleared and I stood on the hill cheering in exaltation. A few Germans soldiers with white flags approached the tanks and after a few moments were walking in front of the tanks into the town. Windows were thrown open and white bed sheets used as flags of surrender flapped in the breeze.

Soon the British Army liberated Beckdorf. Their trucks

arrived, loaded with food. For the first time I tasted Spam and liked it. That evening I went to the farm and brought mother back to the camp with me. The British officers told us that we would be moved to a safer location in a few days, under British jurisdiction.

The days before we were moved were days of vigilantism. There was no stopping some of the POWs and forced laborers from making true "an eye for an eye." All the Germans in the area stayed locked in their houses. I myself, along with some friends, sought the camp manager who had beaten my mother; but he had anticipated what may be coming and had run off.

Some older men from the camp went looking for a farmer whom they had witnessed seriously injuring a downed American pilot by stabbing him in the back with a pitchfork. They found his farm and although they left his family unharmed, they shot and killed him, then burned his home and all outbuildings on his land.

Almost as soon as we were taken out of the camp in trucks, the Germans moved in and burned it to the ground. They didn't want any evidence to the world—or reminders to themselves—of the brutality and inhuman conditions suffered by the thousands of people who had been their prisoners.

There were 20,000 people at our displaced persons camp, sorted by nationality. When it was our turn to be interviewed, mother claimed Polish nationality and we were grouped with those refugees.

Now that concerns for daily survival were less immediate, my thoughts turned to my brothers and my father. I wondered what might have become of them and if or when we might ever see them again. Father particularly was in mother's thoughts.

During the six months following the end of the war, displaced persons were transported to numerous camps. In the zone controlled by the British there were four million alone and deciding what to do with them had become an almost overwhelming problem. Our group of Polish DPs was moved to a camp called Adelheide. Mother managed to find employment there as a cook, preparing food for children and pregnant women. Henry Mazurek, the food supervisor, also had a job for me: I was in charge of crackers, which I distributed to block managers throughout the building. He and his wife even invited me with them to attend a Polish movie based on the novel *Znachor.* I thought the film was beautiful, but since my comprehension of the Polish language was spotty, I could only under-

*Arthur and Josephine at Camp Adelheide.*

stand about a third of it. I told Henry that I was sorry I could not understand it all, so Henry gave me the novel. After reading the novel three times and with Henry tutoring me in grammar, I had a good command of Polish which made me more acceptable to the Poles.

Mother and I were soon on the move again. During our transport to another DP camp we met the Kowalewicz family—John, the father, a son and three daughters. I spent a lot of time with the family, mostly playing cards with the son, John Jr., who was about my age. I liked the teenage daughter, Olga, as well. We went dancing one warm July night. The next day she was very ill; vomiting and feverish. Mother helped look after her, but her condition deteriorated. She and Olga's father decided to take her to the doctor. Mother thought Olga should be hospitalized, but the doctor said she would do better at home.

She died a few days later apparently of encephalitis, a brain infection. Her death alone would have been sad enough, but it was made even sadder by the fact that she had previously lost her mother and had managed to survive the brutal war years. It seemed such a tragedy.

Soviet officers had begun visiting the DP camps, gathering up the Soviet citizens to transport them back to the U.S.S.R. General Eisenhower's soldiers had to force many people at bayonet point into the transports that would carry them back. Eisenhower was complying with Stalin's orders. Many Soviet citizens would do anything to avoid returning to the Soviet Union. John Kowalewicz and I witnessed some poor souls who drank wood alcohol to commit suicide. When discovered, they were placed on bare bunks where they would lie while their insides were eaten away. In his book *The Politian*, an underground publication of the John Birch Society, Robert Welch later described these very events that we witnessed.

Mother had claimed Polish citizenship for two reasons. First, after the arrest of father, there was no way she wanted any part of communist life. Second, she was aware that once we returned, we would be placed in a labor camp. Two of the Soviet officers eventually came to mother, questioning her claim of Polish citizenship. Fortunately, a Jewish French officer intervened on our behalf and told them we did not have to go.

"And why not?" asked one of the officers.

"Why should I return to the country who took my husband and sent him to Siberia even though he worked so hard for the government and cared for his family?" replied mother.

"You do not love your country! You are nothing but a traitor!" shouted the other officer.

"My country? That was never my country. I was born in Poland and I will stay here with my people!" mother cried.

The Soviet officers moved toward mother, but the French officer stood his ground. "You will not take her from my camp!" he told them emphatically.

The Russians grumbled briefly and left. When they returned to their car, they discovered it had been turned upside down. The French officer tried not to laugh, but he could not contain himself. British officers had to provide an escort for the Soviets to ensure them a safe departure.

We were moved again, this time to a camp named Marx. I found work in the food distribution center. I would dispense food to block managers, the amount based on how many people were in their section. While there I had the opportunity to play ping pong at the YMCA and was eventually selected by the camp manager to attend a YMCA training

*The certificate Art received at the completion*
*of his YMCA leadership training.*

camp to be trained as a youth leader. Here I learned the value of responsibility and how to interact well with others.

The YMCA camp was made up of several hundred youths of five or six different nationalities. We attended classes and learned to play a variety of games and sports, many of which I had never seen—such as basketball. At the conclusion of our training we were given diplomas entitling us to be Youth Leaders.

When I returned to Marx, I was given the key to the YMCA building and was put in charge of passing out soccer equipment to the team, an added bonus since soccer was my favorite sport. Mother was once again a cook, this time for the girl's school in Marx.

I attended two classes while I was there: catechism and driver's training. The catechism class was conducted by a priest. When I was through I was able to make my First Communion. At age eighteen I was the oldest in my class, but this was the first opportunity I had to receive any religious training.

The driver's training class was taught by a German civil driver's training instructor. Anyone who completed the class and passed would be entitled to drive both cars and trucks. The course fee was two packs of cigarettes. There was a shortage of many commodities at this time and cigarettes were very valuable. The ration was one carton per person per month. I used mine to barter for other goods. Coffee was also in demand and a person could by a fairly decent automobile for ten pounds of it.

I paid my two pack fee and started my instruction. The first lesson lasted five minutes and I learned to shift gears. The second lasted just as long and I learned to drive and steer. On day three—presto! I had my license.

The DP camps in Germany each housed more than 30,000 people. In spite of the fact that only about three hundred jobs were available per camp, mother and I were always employed. Although we were paid no money for the work, we received double rations. The food distributed was low in quality and quantity—pea soup almost every day accompanied by a slice of bread. C.A.R.E. packages from America were a huge bonus. As workers, we received two; when barrels of clothing arrived from the United States, workers not only had first choice, but could also have two of everything.

I really didn't enjoy being idle. Like many other youths, I hungered for the opportunity to do something creative, something different. I had spent so much valuable time slaving for the Nazis that now I was invigorated and enthusiastic, eager to learn as much as possible. I seemed to always be in high gear. Any opportunity to work gave me a feeling of value, a sense of being useful.

The United Nations Refugee Relief Association (UNRRA) gradually took more responsibility for the DP camps away from the military. They posted a large sign in their office saying that they needed drivers who were able to move to a separate camp and live there. I discussed it with mother and we decided that it would be a good opportunity for me. I was hired and given a special UNRRA driver's license, then sent to their school to learn detailed driving and mechanics before being relocated to Verden.

Verden was a very small camp consisting of only one housing block, but the living conditions there were better than those of the other camps where we had stayed. It was only half a mile away from the UNRRA office.

My first assignment was to transport a few workers in a five-ton Dodge truck to a forest. The workers would cut trees and load them into the truck to be delivered to different camps for firewood. I was quite happy with my new assignment.

The UNRRA carpool consisted of ten trucks, two ambulances, and an old red 1928 Adler convertible. The

English sergeant in charge of the motor pool took a liking to me and soon reassigned me to the old Adler. My new assignment was as a chauffeur to Miss Crisp, the officer in charge of schools in three of the DP camps. This was much more pleasant than driving a truck filled with wood. The job also required that I dress in a professional manner. Miss Crisp took me to a warehouse where I chose stylish, quality apparel suitable for my new position.

In bad weather Miss Crisp preferred the safety of a truck. I took a cue from her one wintry day when I had to pick up another woman who worked for the UNRRA. On the way back to the camp as I was inching slowly over an icy road, the truck began to skid. It went off the road and slid down an embankment, then fell over on its side. Neither of us was injured. Only the woman's clothing was ruined from leaky battery acid. The two of us found shelter in an old train station until another driver could come to pick her up. The stationmaster fed me some chicken soup before I left to stay with the truck until help arrived. I nearly froze during the wait. There were so many accidents that day it took nearly eight hours for someone to get to my truck for assistance.

Early in the spring of 1946 Miss Crisp took the two-week leave she had earned. As her driver, I accompanied her to an officer's resort in Bavaria. It was my first vacation. There was mineral water to drink and I was served five meals a day in the sergeant's mess. It was the best food I had ever eaten. With the combination of the food and the pure mountain air, I returned to Germany rejuvenated.

One evening an ambulance driver asked me to substitute for him for a few hours because he and his wife wanted to attend a dance. Since there were usually few emergencies on a Saturday night I agreed. About 10:00 p.m. there was a call to pick up a woman at Marx, about seven miles away. When I got there I discovered she was pregnant and had to go to the hospital to deliver—a twenty-five mile trip. Halfway there she began screaming for me to pull over because she was delivering her child. Fortunately for me, she knew exactly what to do. I'm sure she would have been embarrassed if she knew that I was not a qualified medic. I followed her instructions and cut and tied off the umbilical cord. When it was over and she was settled, I resumed the trip to the hospital, still a bit shaken. It was the first and last time I ever agreed to substitute for an ambulance driver.

The Kowalewicz family was now in Sande, a camp where Miss Crisp had duties. This gave me the opportunity to visit with them. John's daughter, Catherine, had married and now lived there with her new husband, Alex, who amused us all when he wore his storyteller hat. I saw that Mr. Kowalewicz was very industrious and able to provide more and better food for his family than most. He was an excellent barterer and, for the length of my stay, insisted that I share in their meals.

On Easter Sunday in 1947, a Bishop Gawlina from Canada visited Germany for a special celebration of peace in Europe. Each branch of the service occupying Germany at the time was to be represented at the ceremony. There was one officer representing the Polish officers and I was chosen to represent the Polish servicemen under

*Bishop Gawlina of Canada*

British command. Since this was the largest celebration since the end of the war, the towns in Deutschland were decorated in full regalia in honor of the bishop's visit. A portion of his speech encouraged everyone to work for peace in the world. He told the youth present that they were the hope for the future.

I was uplifted by his message and stood proudly amid the dignitaries, proud to be a Pole—and free.

The following year Miss Crisp arranged for me to attend a newly

*Art's unit of Polish servicemen attached to the British army.*

established trade school in Hanover. There was a warehouse full of metalworking machines which had originally belonged to Poland but were stolen by the Nazis and it seemed to make good sense to put them to use training young men as tool and die makers.

When I returned, I found that many of my friends had emigrated to other countries; the Kowalewiczs included. Unfortunately, a mother and a son did not constitute a family according to the immigration rules of countries such as the U.S.,

*The tool and die section of the trade school in Hanover.*

Canada, Brazil and Argentina. These countries wanted young people. Since mother was now fifty-eight, she would need a sponsor in one of those countries and there was none for her.

Again Miss Crisp came to the rescue and assisted us. She located a hospital in Scotland that was looking for a cleaning lady and helped mother emigrate there to fill the position. She said we could worry about my emigration later.

Since the British Army was looking for volunteers to replace their soldiers, I decided to join the Civilian Military Labor Organization (CMLO) rather than drive for Miss Crisp. The Berlin blockade had created a demand for at least 4,000 truck drivers, and I was one of those chosen to train drivers and inspect their trucks. The training school was in Cuxhaven, which was located on a North Sea inlet to the port of Hamburg. There the trainees and instructors shared the barracks, each in their own section. Engines of trucks operating in support of the blockade were never shut off. Drivers slept at the wheel while the trucks were loaded with medical supplies and other items, such as coal. When fully loaded, the trucks were driven to their respective unloading areas. This gave drivers an opportunity to change into fresh clothes, grab something to eat, and head back for another load.

I next went to motorcycle school to be trained to lead truck convoys carrying all types of explosive cargo—even nitroglycerine. The convoys never stopped for traffic signals, much to the chagrin of German police officers, and their speed depended on what type of explosives were being transported: a snail's pace was required for nitroglycerine.

After my stint

*Arthur's motorcycle troop.*

99

with the convoys, the CMLO sent me to Nienburg to drive for a Captain Johns, the commanding officer of that organization. He had served as a judge during the Nuremberg Trial. I tried my utmost to please the captain by dressing well and snapping to attention whenever I had to open his door. We got along very well. Sometimes his visits to the officers' club could get a bit tedious for me, particularly if I had to wait to the wee hours of the morning. Occasionally I would have to help the captain into the house and settle him on the couch for the rest of the night.

Captain Johns was very appreciative because I didn't complain about the long waits outside the club while he was inside socializing, so he would try to make it up to me. Many times because of his delays I would be late for soccer matches. The captain would then tell me to take his car, a black Mercedes, to the game. He knew I would feel like a big shot since no other drivers were given the same privilege—and he was right.

The captain's wife had been expecting a baby. It was delivered at home by a midwife, then an ambulance took the mother and newborn son to the hospital for an examination. Just before the ambulance arrived, I brought a bouquet of flowers to Mrs. Johns. I was quite pleased when she chose my flowers over the many others she had received to take with her to the hospital. When she left, I drove Captain Johns straight to the officer's club with a box of cigars.

In the late summer of 1950 I was transferred again. The British needed qualified people to drive 36-wheel trailers to transport army tanks. Some of the bridges I had to cross were built post-war and were of limited capacity, not strong enough to support a loaded trailer.

In order to cross, the tank had to be removed from the trailer and driven slowly across the bridge. The trailer would be driven across next. It was slow, tedious work, but with it came a thirty percent increase in pay and could be gratifying, particularly when left to my own devices. It helped, too, when the supervisors recognized my initiative and expressed their satisfaction.

I continued to make new friends in the camp. Marion Zwiersczowski was a woodworker who was born in the Ukraine near the Polish border. His village was devastated in the fighting between German and Soviet troops. We spent many hours playing cards and discussing the war.

The Galaska's from Warsaw were my adopted family. Mr Galaska was a decorator with three beautiful daughters. I was interested in the oldest of the three, Stela, but Mr. and Mrs. Galaska were quite protective. Whenever I courted Stela, the two younger sisters were there as chaperones. The three girls were immensely popular; their one-room apartment at the camp was usually full of young people seeking their company. Later in the year the family emigrated to Boston and was sorely missed by everyone—especially me.

Another young German girl, Mousie, working as a telephone operator piqued my interest. She and I would have long phone conversations but she refused to meet me in person because her father was quite bitter about the outcome of the war. Eventually she gave in and agreed to meet me outside a theater. We began dating, but I was only allowed to visit her in the parlor when her father wasn't home. He would never stand for his daughter dating a Pole. Because of that, and the fact that I wanted to leave Germany at my first opportunity, our romance was doomed from the start.

So many people had emigrated to England after the war that the country could accept no more. British soldiers were returning home and in need of jobs. The terrible Italian Coal Mine Riot left many British subjects injured and sparked bad feelings towards immigrants in general.

I was disheartened upon learning that the English borders were closed to immigration. Mother had written to me many times over the past two years proclaiming the kindness of the Scottish people and the merits of the country.

As with most rules there are always exceptions, so it was with the rules regarding immigration to England. There were special cases when it was still allowed. Many Polish pilots had escaped from Poland during the war and had, in turn, flown for the British Air Force. Those who were wounded were placed in a special International Camp in England.

With Captain John's influence, I was assigned to the International camp to work. Sponsored by the Friends of Polish Veterans (SPK), on April 6, 1951, I left the Port of Hamburg. Few of my friends were left behind; most had already emigrated to other parts of the world: the United States, Canada, South America and even Australia. I thought of them as I crossed the churning North Sea.

# Chapter 13

# Scottish Education

*"You must do the thing you think you cannot do."*

—*Eleanor Roosevelt*

From London I traveled by train to Dundee, Scotland. I was impressed with the efficiency and courtesy of the train master and the conductors. In England and Germany the people were gracious—Ms. Crisp, Captain Johns and the British people had treated me and other displaced persons with consideration and respect. The Scottish people followed suit and were nice as well.

What I didn't know about the English language could fill the proverbial library, but I managed to get by. On the train I met a Scottish gentleman who engaged me in conversation about the war. I was slightly amused by his kilt since I had never seen one before. His destination was also Dundee and he suggested that when we arrive at the station I follow him through a shortcut to avoid the crowds. It worked and I gratefully thanked him and said goodbye.

Mother and I planned to meet at the Polish Ex-Serviceman's Club in Dundee. It was a little piece of Poland of sorts where Poles found comfort in socializing with their own people.

I took a taxi to the club. I looked around briefly but did not see her. I went in an identified myself to the husband and wife who managed the club, Joseph and Anna Gutbier. They were aware of our planned reunion and took me into the kitchen where a dinner was waiting for me.

Mother came in while I was eating and was overjoyed to see me. Her tears mingled with her smile. She explained that she had found a man to take her to the train station to meet me but obviously we had missed each other.

I was indeed happy to be with her again, too. For all she knew, her youngest son was the only one to have survived the war. And no one had heard anything of father since the night he was taken away.

I took a sleeping room upstairs at the club and began hunting for employment. There was a Polish newspaper which was published in England listing jobs available. These jobs, however, were the leftovers—those that the Scots didn't want, that the Poles had no choice but to take if they wanted to earn a living.

My first job was in a carpet mill where I operated a giant machine which applied a sticky glue solution to the backing of carpets. Another part of my job was to handsaw the carpet into various sizes—painstaking work.

A Polish immigrant named Frank was my coworker and trainer. After a couple of months the two of us broke the standing production record and received written recognition from the management. We took pride in our work and it was apparent to the people who mattered.

Even though my job was that of a laborer, I always dressed up before going to the factory where I would change into my work clothes. And when the workday was done, I would change back before leaving the building. The sting I felt remembering how, as a forced laborer in Germany, people would move away from me on the train because of my smell and shabby appearance, had deeply affected me. I now had the ability to take care of myself and I did so.

While I was employed at the carpet factory I began dating a stunning woman, Nancy, a couple of years my senior. She was a carpet designer who worked in the offices with management and had the title Doctor of Design bestowed upon her with the publication of a book she had written about the subject. Her family owned some supermarkets and theaters in Scotland.

Even though Nancy didn't mind that I had no formal education or wealth, I never felt comfortable around her parents and educated friends. Although her well-bred Scottish family was very charming and did their best to make me feel at ease whenever I visited, their home was a mansion and I felt out of place. Nancy's father even offered to train me in business if she and I should marry. We dated for several months but because of my discomfort, the relationship cooled off and ended.

On our days off, mother and I would send letters to Kiev, Poland and even Boston, Massachusetts, in an effort to get news of our relatives. We had heard nothing in years. Father's two brothers and two sisters had emigrated to the United States from Riga, Latvia in 1914. None of mother's family knew she had survived the war or that she was now living in Scotland.

While working in the hospital, mother befriended a patient who had been a Polish officer and was now married to the daughter of a retired Scottish admiral. He and mother conversed often in Polish. Both he and his wife loved Polish cuisine and hired mother to cook full-time for them. She moved out of her sleeping room and into the couple's estate in the country. She soon had a garden to enjoy and she was able to watch the horses graze in the meadow through her kitchen window. I was welcome anytime, even to stay overnight if my work schedule permitted.

The carpet factory closed for two weeks each year to

give everyone a vacation. Since I had nowhere else to go, I spent my two weeks on the estate with mother. During one of my daily walks to the nearby village I decided to call the Polish club to see if I had any mail. Anna answered the phone and told me that I had received a letter from a Mr. Arthur Berg in Boston. I knew it must have been a response to one of the many inquiry letters mother and I had sent out in an attempt to trace our relatives. The last correspondence our family had received from relatives in the U.S. was a letter to my father in 1926. Excitedly, I asked Anna to read it to me over the phone and sure enough, it was a response to my letter to Emily, father's sister, Arthur Berg's mother.

The Red Cross had been trying to locate Emily for mother for the past seven years without success. I took it upon myself to write to the postmaster of Jamaica Plains, Massachusetts, to see if I could locate the "lost" aunt. As it happened, Emily had been widowed and then married a man named Kigel. The postmaster remembered an Emily Berg from years before on a previous route, so he had the letter delivered to her son, Arthur Berg. In his letter to me, Arthur asked for more details about me and mother and so a correspondence began.

Something else also began in the back of my mind— a tiny bud of hope. Could it be? Was America in my future?

About this time, the Polish Ex-Serviceman's Club in Dundee was about to be sold. It would be a great loss to the Polish residents who relied on the club for a great deal of their socializing. The Gutbiers had emigrated and the new management was unable to keep the operation of the club profitable; something needed to be done.

During one of the meetings to discuss the matter, I stated that the committee had hired the wrong people to manage the club—a former Polish mayor and a retired Polish officer who knew nothing of business. Times were changing and ranks and titles no longer meant much. Practical business sense was what mattered if the club was to be saved.

The committee suggested electing someone on a temporary basis to manage the club to see if things would work out. They elected me.

I had no idea if I could handle the position. Mother encouraged me to try since the two of us had always sought opportunities to progress. She said she would even give up her comfortable position at the estate to help me. I decided to do it.

The decision turned out to be the best I ever made. It gave me invaluable business experience which I put to good use throughout my life.

The club had a library consisting of about 2,000 books written in Polish and was a great educational and entertainment resource for all who visited there. The sleeping rooms available for rent were only partially occupied when I took over. In order to fill those remaining I made trips to the farms in the surrounding area where Poles worked as hired hands, putting in long hours for little pay. With my good reputation at the factory, I was able to get them work there. The managers knew Poles were hard workers and trusted my recommendations. Since these new factory workers needed living quarters nearby, the club was a logical choice. Soon all the rooms were rented.

The men living at the club had no families in Dundee and regarded the club as their home and treated it as such. They voluntarily cleaned up the yard and planted flowers and bushes. Their pride in their home extended to the inside as well. They painted the interior and made the whole building much more inviting. Across the street from the club was the residence of an Anglican bishop and there was an unofficial contest of sorts between the bishop's full-time gardner and the club residents to see who could boast the best looking garden—a green-thumbathon, if you will.

Mother cooked two meals a day of mainly traditional

Polish dishes when she was able to find the right ingredients.

As the club's membership flourished, I started a chess club which attracted not only the usual members, but also a great number of Scots as well. Drinks were reasonably priced and many gentlemen would come in each evening for a few drinks and a leisurely game of chess.

There was a Scottish farmer who frequented the club and routinely picked up leftover table scraps for the pigs on his farm. This gave me an idea. I would make him a business proposition the next time he came in.

"How many pigs do you have?" I asked him.

"One hundred and twenty," he replied.

"Would you consider selling me one of them?"

He hesitated. "It is just too risky. You know meat is rationed. A sale like this would be considered trafficking in black market goods. If I am caught..."

"I'll give you thirty pounds."

"It would have to be at least fifty..."

"Thirty-six and you kill it and back up the truck and drop it off."

He thought for a moment and accepted this offer.

A few days later the pig was delivered, at night, handed through the kitchen window in the rear of the building. I was already prepared for the next step. Just after closing the deal with the farmer I had gone to an old, unused outhouse at the back of the property and built a small concrete fireplace inside, then sealed the small building. It was now a smokehouse.

Since mother had been raised on a pig farm in Poland, she knew how to butcher the animal. Next, she solicited my help and the help of one of the boarders who was the son of a butcher. The three of us worked through the night making sausages, hams and bacon. Then we secretly cured the meat in the new smokehouse. This arrangement became a regular and profitable occurrence for both the farmer and me.

After closing one night I was cleaning up the bar when two bobbies came in to have a look around. There were very strict rules about not selling alcohol after 10:00 pm, but the bar was empty except for me. Then one of them looked up and saw the Polish sausages hanging from broomsticks above the bar.

"My, aren't you lucky to be able to import sausage from Poland," he said.

"Certainly lucky, that he is," said the other.

I didn't say anything; I just held my breath.

They glanced at each other. "Well, good night," they said and walked out.

Something told me they knew what was going on; maybe it was the twinkle in their eyes. If they did know, they didn't let on because I never heard anymore about it. I thought about what would have happened to someone in the Soviet Union who was suspected of dealing in the black market. My admiration for the British and the Scots increased.

Sugar was another rationed necessity. I received an allotted amount based on how many cups of tea were served at the club each month. Just down the street from the club was a bakery and the baker and I

*Arthur at the Polish Ex-Serviceman's Club in Dundee*

had become friends. Bakeries used a lot of sugar for their confectionary products, and the baker found that he was allotted more sugar than he needed, so he shared it with me. I had all I needed, so I never bothered to pick up my allotment at the local store. After a couple of months an inspector showed up at the club and asked me if I would please go and pick up my allotment of sugar because I was giving them cause for speculation.

I was amazed by the politeness of the inspector. I could not help but remember how I had to shop with mother back at the government store in Kiev. Scotland was a one-hundred and eighty degree turn.

As I club manager I learned invaluable business, one of the most important being: *Listen carefully to your salesman*. For example, a liquor salesman explained which brand of whiskey to purchase for the bar: it was the brand that had an extra shot per bottle. He then suggested that if I turn the bottle upside down when it was empty, another half of a shot would drip out. Another lesson: *Never waste anything*. The salesman also knew what the competition was doing in terms of business and passed along some trade secrets, also valuable. I learned to always make time for salesmen no matter where or with which business I was involved.

# Chapter 14

# Ready for Success

*"Chance is always powerful. Let your*
*hook be always cast; in the pool*
*where you least expect it, there will be*
*a fish.*

—*Ovid*

Life was certainly better in Scotland than it had been
after the war in Germany, and better than in the U.S.S.R. in
ways too numerous to mention. But I knew that if I really
wanted to be a success I had to enter the Land of
Opportunity—the United States. Somewhat of a class struc-
ture existed in Scotland and England. For instance, if a person
was born into a family of physicians, becoming a physician
was relatively easy. But without such a birthright any type of
upward mobility was quite difficult.

We received information that mother's sisters and
brothers had survived the war; however, things were not very
good in Poland now that it was ruled by a communist government. Mother began a lifelong habit of sending packages
of goods to her relatives. The government in Poland did not
persecute families for having contact with persons in the
West as did the communists in the U.S.S.R.

I had begun corresponding not only with cousin
Berg, but also with my two elderly aunts. They wished to help
me, their brother's son, come to America. My father, Joseph,

had been the only one of their siblings who had not left Riga but instead stayed behind to attend the University of Riga to become an engineer. No one could have foreseen what horrific events would unfold upon those people who remained in or near Russia.

The day came when documents of sponsorship arrived from Aunt Emily and Aunt Minnie in Boston. They had also included a check for $200 to pay for passage by ocean liner from Southampton, England, to New York City. I now had all I needed to go to America—except for a visa.

The American Embassy was in Glasglow which was about a hundred miles from Dundee. I had to travel there by train and spend the night. I was twenty-six and it was my first time in a hotel.

When I arrived at the embassy, the receptionist informed me that there was no way I could see the consul without an appointment. Disheartened, I lolled about, trying to come up with a solution to my predicament.

I noticed that there was a steady stream of people completely bypassing the receptionist and going further back into the building. I went outside for a short while, then returned and marched quickly through the reception area and down a corridor until I came to the consul's office. I walked in.

The consul was surprised but polite. He asked how he could help me, so I explained my situation to him. He took my papers and looked them over.

"I'm sorry, but you are Polish and the quota of Polish immigrants is exhausted for the next five years," he said.

The look of despair on my face must have been very evident to him.

"Just a minute," he said. He took my papers and left the room. In a few minutes he returned.

"I think I may have a solution to your problem," he said.

I leaned forward, on the edge of my chair.

"You were born in Kiev, Ukraine. Why don't we list you as a Ukrainian National? They still have open quotas."

I was ready to genuflect to this man and kiss his hand. Emigrating to America was no easy matter during this period. The Gutbiers had waited seven years for immigration papers.

When I returned to the club I told my story to some of the regulars. One of the boarders said that he had also received some papers from the embassy, but he didn't understand what they meant. He was from a small farm town and never had an opportunity for a formal education. Evidently he had just shoved them in a drawer where they remained for several months.

"Bring them to me. I'll take a look at them," I said.

When he handed them to me I knew what they were: his papers allowing him to immigrate to the United States. He had no idea what he possessed.

As word spread around the club, I found there were others in situations similar to this man—men who had worked hard all their lives just to have the bare necessities, with no time for much of an education. Most had never held a job before and did not know how to handle a regular income. I decided to do something to help them. Each week I had them give me a portion of their pay which I deposited in the bank for them. When they needed money for a new suit or for traveling, I would withdraw that amount for them. It was the only way they could keep from spending every last hard-earned cent.

While I was making my plans to leave Scotland, mother and I received a letter from Zan. Her favorite son was alive. She couldn't have been more excited. Of all the letters I had written to different addresses in the Ukraine only one had apparently gotten through. It was to my friend Vassily, the forest ranger. Vassily's son ran to Zan's apartment the minute the family read my letter.

I learned from Zan that Darnica had been annihilated by the Germans when they pulled out of Kiev. He thought mother and I had perished in Poland, never dreaming that we had been sidetracked to the German labor camps. Zan was exhilarated to know that we had survived. He was married to Nadia and now had three children: Valerie, Henry and Anna. Anatole was also alive and he and Hala had two children, Vladimir and Zana. But my closest brother, Henry, was killed in 1943 near Harkov while taking pictures of the front lines in battle.

Mother felt blessed. I felt that someday I would see my brothers again. This feeling of a reunion someday warmed me deeply inside.

One concern I had before going was that the club would be in good, capable hands after I left. To make sure it was I had a dear friend, Mietek, help me out with the day-to-day operation. Mietek had his mother, sister and other relatives in Dundee help him out. I was confident that they would do a fine job and that the committee would be relieved of the chore of finding and training someone new.

When I handed the operation over to Mietek, mother retired with a small pension. Additionally, I left her all of our savings less twenty dollars to pay for my transportation from New York to Boston.

The Polish Veterans Club Committee invited me to their headquarters in London for a farewell tea. They were most pleased because the success of the club kept them from having to sell it. The president of the committee told me that, because of my persistence and thoroughness, I must pursue establishing my own business in the United States. Polish newspapers throughout Scotland ran articles praising the Dundee Club stating, "If anyone wants to learn how to manage a club, go visit Art Lukowski's club in Dundee."

On March 13, 1954, I boarded her majesty's ship, the

Queen Elizabeth I, which embarked from Southampton. Destination: New York City.

My American Life

# Chapter 15

# Across the Sea to the West

*"There is no security in this life. There is only opportunity."*

—*Douglas MacArthur*

The Queen Elizabeth I was a mammoth ship, a very impressive vehicle to transport me on my journey to a freedom such as I had never before known. I shared a cabin on a lower level with three other men. It was a tight fit; the four of us could not stand all at once. But the only time I spent in the cabin was for sleeping. After I deposited my bag there I began exploring this city afloat.

Making friends was simple since I spoke three and a half languages, the half being English. At my dining room table were members of a British circus enroute to Ohio for a performance: four beautiful women, a magician, a midget, and two more entertainers. I danced with the ladies, as did other gentlemen there, and had a grand time. Our table was the most popular in the dining room because of the circus girls.

The following evening a gentleman from the first class section invited the girls to join his party. The women accepted with the condition that everyone at the table would be welcome. He agreed, and we were all entertained in the first class dancing hall. The host paid the band to play overtime until 5:00 a.m. and had champagne served all the while. His bill for the party was $1,800, an amount that seemed astronomical to me at the time.

It wasn't long before the seas got a bit choppy and many passengers got seasick. For some reason, I remained unaffected. When I went into the dining room for breakfast, it was empty. The waiter arrived to take my order. Almost jokingly I asked for six eggs. "Most certainly, sir," he answered. Food in Scotland was still rationed and each person was only allowed two eggs per week. This was the first time I was able to have as much food as I could eat.

One morning I was approached by a man who heard that I was trilingual. It seemed his roommate had been bedridden for three days and would neither talk nor get up. He thought I might be able to communicate with him to find out what was wrong.

I went with him and spoke to the man and learned that he was a Russian Jew with an Israeli passport. The man had hydrophobia. His roommate and I managed to coax him into taking a shower. I brought him some food then we took him to the barber to make him presentable. His outlook improved and he was much calmer after that.

It was the last evening of the cruise and most everyone aboard was too excited to sleep. We were all anxious to view the French Lady in New York Harbor as she welcomed us with her torch aglow. For so many of us tomorrow would be the first time we had ever set foot on this new, unfamiliar soil of America to become part of a new culture. We were filled with hope.

After I disembarked, I realized now that I was alone here on the streets of New York. I wished I would have had someone waiting to meet me when the ship docked.

Soon I found a taxi and asked the driver the rate to Grand Central Station via Radio City Music Hall, one of two places I had always wanted to see; the other was Niagara Falls.

The driver said the fare would be $3.50, but he offered me a deal: a short tour around various other landmarks as well for $5.00. I took it.

I was in awe of the monumental buildings I saw on that short taxi tour. I was also amazed at the impulsive, impetuous and seemingly unpatterned way the taxi driver maneuvered through the rush-rush world.

Radio City Music Hall was all that I hoped it would be, a sight through the taxi window I will never forget. Many of my friends and I thought *everything* having to do with entertainment came from there. We had never heard of a place called Hollywood.

# Chapter 16

## Americanization

*"For anything worth having,*
*One must pay the price;*
*And the price is always work,*
*patience, love, self-sacrifice."*

*—John Burroughs*

When I arrived at Grand Central Station, I sent a telegram to my aunt that I was on my way, then boarded the train to Boston. I was hungry, so I went to the dining car and ordered my first fried chicken dinner and a bottle of Schlitz. I chose Schlitz because I had seen a sign advertising it.

The train arrived in Boston and I got off. I looked around and saw two little old ladies anxiously waiting at the end of the platform. I approached them and one asked, "Are you Art?"

"Yes," I said. It turned out that she was Aunt Emily. We hugged for a long while, then she looked me over.

"Oh, you look so much like Joseph when he was young," she said.

I smiled, but my smile was touched with sadness. I felt sad for these ladies who had no idea what had become of their brother and sad for myself as well; I was missing a father.

That evening, March 18, 1954, there was a double celebration at the Berg's home—one for my arrival and one for Aunt Emily's birthday.

Aunt Emily was kind enough to give me free room and board, making certain that I ate a hot meal each day. She knew I needed employment, so she suggested that I work as a doorman because for the lucrative tips. This didn't appeal to me because I was more interested in business, so I kept looking and managed to get a job for minimum wage in an ornament manufacturing company.

It didn't take long for me to notice the large amount of waste involved in the production process. I even handed out some of the damaged ornaments to the neighborhood children who played outside the building. The primary reason ornaments were classified as rejects was because of the different colors on the pieces running together and spoiling the design. I studied the manufacturing operations and after about three weeks, discovered that most of the spoiled ornaments could be eliminated by extending the drying process. I simply applied the lesson I had learned about waste from the liquor salesman at the club in Scotland. The owner of the company was so impressed that he decided to train me as a foreman.

I discovered that the Galaskas, the family with the three beautiful daughters that I had known at the DP camps in Germany, had immigrated to Boston. When I contacted them I learned that the three daughters had each married, had children, and still lived near their parents' home. They invited me over and it was a heartwarming reunion. They treated me as they always had—as a son and a brother.

Marion Zwierszowski and I had also kept in touch with one another. He had written that if I ever made it to America I should look him up and he would take me on a two-week vacation—his treat. I contacted Marion and took him up on his offer. It meant that I would have to quit my job since I hadn't yet earned any vacation time. I gave my boss the appropriate notice and he told me that I was always welcome back.

Marion arrived and I was ready. We planned a trip to Canada through Niagara Falls and then on to Ontario for a visit with the Baranowski family, which included my god-daughter. We chose a route that took us through Detroit where my Uncle Casmir "Cass" Pokorski lived. Uncle Cass was my mother's youngest brother. In 1914 she had walked with him to the border of Poland and Germany to help him escape being drafted into the Tsar's army. While saying goodbye, she gave him five gold rubles—a large sum then and all the money she had.

There was disappointment and the seed of anger growing within me toward Uncle Cass. I had written to him from Scotland asking him to sponsor mother so she could come to the United States, but he never responded. When we did meet and I explained to him the hardships endured by his sister throughout the years, he immediately did the required paperwork for sponsorship.

Marion and I were delighted to see the Ford plants in Detroit. Throughout all of Europe, Detroit was known as *the* automobile production capital of the world. But for me by far the most exciting part of the trip was visiting Chicago, the city to which most of my friends had immigrated and where they had put down roots. Chicago now had a larger Polish population than any other city in the world outside of Warsaw.

Armed with a city map, an address book, and some coins for buses and streetcars, I set off by alone to arrive unannounced to shock my friends; they weren't aware that I was in the country. When I arrived at John Kowalewicz's house, John, John's father and I celebrated all night long. I'd been gone for twenty-four hours and Marion was ready to call the police.

After our vacation I decided to stay in Chicago. I shared an apartment with Marion and Stephen Joseph, near Anna and Joseph Gutbier. Dividing rent, utilities and grocery costs three ways proved to be very economical.

One day while I was out looking for work, I became quite ill. I went back to the apartment with shooting pains in my side. Vomiting soon followed and I found it difficult to leave my bed. Anna prepared healthy soups for me, but they didn't help. Finally an old Polish doctor came over and poked and prodded me. He discovered I had kidney stones and gave me two options: I could go to the hospital to have them surgically removed or try to pass them on my own. Since surgery didn't appeal to me and I had no money for it anyway, I decided to pass them. This meant no salt, walking as much as possible, and drinking a virtual river of water.

I went back out on the streets and found a job at Western Electric as a punch press operator. I still had the stones and there were days that I went to work so sick I could hardly stand. It was several weeks before they finally passed. At the end of each week on payday there was enough money left from my $1.10 per hour paycheck after paying bills for a bottle of whiskey—a few shots before we went to a dance or a movie.

Several months passed and I was settling in to this new country. It was time to seriously consider my future; I needed a plan. The dream of owning a business had never left me. Currently I lived in a Polish neighborhood, shopped at a Polish bakery, heard Mass in Polish—even my foreman at work was Polish. I was not learning enough about *American* culture and if I was to make the United States my permanent home, I should adopt the American way of life. Unfortunately at this point, I wasn't even sure what the typical American way of life really was.

While still employed at Western Electric, I began asking around about various businesses. One night while having a drink at a local Polish tavern, I asked the owner what the worst business to get into was.

"The restaurant business," he answered. "It's the easiest to get into, but half of first time restaurateurs go broke."

*Easiest to get into* was all I needed to hear. Now I needed some experience. Marion volunteered to take me to different parts of Chicago each Sunday to look for any kind of restaurant job. We both knew it would be hard because I lacked a command of the English language. After six or seven weeks of leaving applications all over the city, Marion was about to give up. There was not a single response; it was disheartening.

Then one Sunday in March we pulled into a parking space at Richard's Drive-In Carfateria at 87th and Stoney Island Avenue on Chicago's south side. The place was buzzing and all the help was running around in a frenzy. We watched for a few minutes and saw a couple of cars pull away, their drivers disgusted and out of patience.

It was about 11:00 am when I went inside to apply.

"Come back later. I'm too busy to talk to you now," the manager, Mr. Reiley, told me.

"Right now is when you need help," I said. "If you would be willing to try me out, I'll work for the rest of the day without pay."

*Richard's Drive-In Carfateria in Chicago.*

Mr. Reiley thought for just a moment, then handed me an apron and pointed me to the fountain to begin dispensing

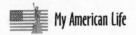 

soft drinks. Marion went home and I worked until closing time at midnight.

As we cleaned up that night Mr. Reiley asked me if I would come back the next day, Monday. He was impressed that I had worked all those hours without a single break. I told him I'd have to give my present employer at least three days notice, and I'd be ready to work full time after that.

Implementation of my plan had begun. I had my first job in an American restaurant. I knew I'd need experience in many types of food services if I was to be a successful restaurant owner.

Thursday of that week I began my career at Richards. The bus trip from my neighborhood to the drive-in took about an hour and forty-five minutes and included several transfers. I arrived early for work each day and stayed late if necessary. It didn't take me long to realize that I was spending too much time in transit. I asked Mr. Reiley if he knew of a rooming house nearby. It so happened that a lady employed in the Richard's chain of restaurants had a single room to let out in her apartment for $10 per week. It was a bare room, but the price was right and I didn't have much leisure time anyway with the long hours I was putting in at the restaurant. When I did have spare time, I liked to read American books and magazines—I didn't need fancy furniture or decorations for that.

I would sometimes arrive at the restaurant before anyone was there to open the doors. One rainy March morning when Mr. Reiley came to open up, he found me drenched to the bone.

"You know, Arthur, you've been an excellent employee," he said once we were inside. "You've learned the soda fountain operation and kitchen procedure as well. I think it's time you had keys to open. I'll send you to take a lie detector test, which is required for anyone with a key. When you pass you'll be able to run the cash register as well."

I was very excited. Unfortunately, when I took the test, I failed. I was shocked! I couldn't imagine...then it hit me. I had indeed lied. When I was asked if I'd ever stolen anything I said no. But I had, out of necessity, years before in Russia—I took the oil and grain. And I had also given out those rejected ornaments to the children playing around the factory in Boston.

I explained those incidents to the administrator of the test and took the test again—and passed.

From the day I received my keys I had the fountain and kitchen set up in the mornings by the time everyone else arrived. They loved it. I used the extra quiet time to study the inventory and teach myself the ordering procedure for the perishables and dry goods. Mr. Reiley was surprised one morning when I handed him a list of what needed to be reordered. This relieved him of some of his managerial responsibilities since he was actually the supervisor who was acting as manager of Richard's 87th Street store because of the shortage of help. But within two weeks I was appointed as store manager—I was on my way.

The policy of the company was to hire only single women or girls for curb service and there always seemed to be a shortage of help in that area. Out of desperation I hired two married women—Tommie McCain and Mary Smith. I had no choice since no one else had applied for the positions. They both proved to be dependable, diligent workers, so I continued this hiring practice. The restaurant began to operate more efficiently and I began to win bonuses in the company's operating costs reduction contests. Company management even changed its hiring policy toward married women. Tommie was appointed the training instructor for all new women hired for curb service in the Chicago restaurants. Mary Smith was promoted to cashier at the Stoney Island Richard's.

One pleasant spring morning Mary said she wanted to

talk to me. Summer break for the school was drawing near, and she asked if I would hire her sister Connie to take her place for the summer so she could stay home with her children. I told Mary to bring her in for an interview.

Connie was seventeen and had come up from southern Illinois to spend the summer with Mary. She had never had a job before, but was anxious to work in the "big city." I liked her and hired her. She took a lie detector test and immediately started work.

She seemed to enjoy the job and, I hoped, to enjoy working for me. I didn't learn until much later that she had told Mary, "I'm going to marry that man."

I was twenty-eight at the time and had started to think about settling down. I asked Connie out for a date and she said yes. That was the beginning of our rather unusual courtship. Many of our dates and evenings together revolved around Richard's. After closing shop we would take some large cups of ice cream and go down to the lakefront to sit and gaze at the Chicago skyline. At other times when some of the Richard's managers were behind in taking their monthly inventories, I would do it while Connie waited for me in the car. I would often come out and find her asleep.

One evening while I was inside taking inventory at the Lincolnwood Richard's, I heard the knob of the back door turning.

"Who's there?" I asked in surprise.

The door swung open and there stood Mr. Smith, the owner of the entire Richard's chain. He was in from California, checking out the stores in the middle of the night to see in what shape the managers left them when they closed up. He knew I wasn't the manager of that store and was curious as to why I was there. When I told him I was helping some of the managers catch up on their inventorying, he was most impressed.

A couple of days later I received a call from the main

office downtown. My presence was requested there for a meeting. When I arrived I was handed a coffee mug with my name on it. Under my name was inscribed the title, "Supervisor."

From that point on I began working from 65 to 80 hour weeks. I was getting my business education in massive amounts. There were many problems in dealing with so many employees. Some nights when I finally returned to my small room, exhausted, I questioned my career choice; but I kept on. The summer ended and Mary came back to work. Connie returned home for school.

Late in 1955, mother at last arrived in New York. Uncle Cass and I drove there together to pick her up. We took her to Detroit where she would stay with Cass until I could set up accommodations for the two of us in Chicago. Uncle Cass disappointed me again when he asked me to pay him for mother's room and board. He was very well off financially and had not seen his sister in forty-one years. I made up my mind then that if I could ever help my family in any way I would do so willingly, without compensation.

The following year Connie returned to Chicago and worked for a patent attorney at the Illinois Institute of Technology. I rented a three room apartment for mother and me and Connie took over the sleeping room that I had left. The two places were within walking distance of each other with a bus stop close enough for Connie to travel to IIT.

That summer Connie and I were engaged. And that summer mother and I shared a savings account.

"Mother, I need some of the $700 from our savings to buy an engagement ring for Connie," I said.

"How much will you need?" mother asked

"$700."

Mother sighed and smiled. "You go ahead and take it. I can see it will make you happy. Besides, I like that young lady."

*Connie's father walks her down the aisle.*

On September 20, 1956, Connie and I were married at her church in Johnston City in southern Illinois. When we returned to Chicago, mother rented a hall for seventy-five guests and did all the cooking for the reception herself, refusing help from anyone who offered. The union of Connie and me meant so much to her that she wanted to do everything herself. We had musicians whom I asked to play for four hours straight rather than six with a break so the dancing would be uninterrupted. It was indeed a joyous occasion.

We needed a bigger place to live and we were charmed, it seemed. There was a Richard's on 95th Street in Oak Lawn. On one side of it stood the Martinique Restaurant and Playhouse and on the other side stood a magnificent, 100 year old, nine room farmhouse, completely furnished with antiques. The owners of the house happened to be friends of mine and were anxious to retire to the sunbelt, so they offered to rent the house to the three of us at a very reasonable rate. We were elated with the deal because of the house's character, location—and price.

# Chapter 17

# Learning the Restaurant Business Firsthand

*"Lots of times you have to pretend to
join a parade in which you're not
really interested in order to get where
you're going."*

—*George Morley*

The demands of the restaurant business, combined with a shortage of help, caused us to downsize our honeymoon to a weekend in downtown Chicago—then back to business.

I was devoting my time to another unit of the Richard's chain, Jeff's Charcoal Broil on Harlem Avenue in Lyons, Illinois. I had no one to relieve me from my duties there, so Connie would come by and help after her job as secretary for the Patent Attorney at the Illinois Institute of Technology and on weekends. We worked day and night.

A couple of blocks from our rented house on 95th street was a closed restaurant called Dutchie's. Always keeping an eye open for an opportunity, I spoke to the building's owner, a Mr. Shoemaker. He was a butcher and had failed with the restaurant, but had kept an apartment in the back. With little money to invest, I had to do some creative thinking, and came up with a deal to offer Mr. Shoemaker. If he would get the restaurant in shape to reopen, I'd manage it and we'd split the profits. Mr. Shoemaker agreed and soon Dutchie's reopened

while Connie and I still maintained our regular jobs.

With every day business grew and our efforts and long hours seemed worthwhile. Before long, though, the management of Richard's got word of my side enterprise and gave me an ultimatum: devote my full time and energy to Richard's or quit. I was very grateful to the people at Richard's for the experience I'd received while in their employ but I felt it was time to move on. I resigned my supervisory position.

I could now focus completely on Dutchie's. Connie worked there on evenings and weekends. It wasn't long before Mr. Shoemaker and his wife began to show up in the restaurant more and more with the idea of having a greater presence in the business. They did live in the attached apartment after all and it was next to impossible for them to stay away. Then a conflict arose between Mr. Shoemaker and the help.

Both Mr. Shoemaker and I realized that something wasn't working—something had to give. Since the Shoemakers owned the building, what gave was Connie and I. Mr. Shoemaker bought out my share of the business. With the improvements in the operation that I had made, the business remained open for many years after my departure.

It was now two years since Connie and I had been married and there was finally time for a real honeymoon. While we were making plans where to go, I got a phone call from a Mr. Payne. Mr. Payne owned industrial cafeterias on several factories as well as Braho's Coffee Shop in downtown Hammond, IN. He felt acquiring the coffee shop had been a mistake. All his cafeterias were profitable, but the coffee shop was a loser. He needed someone to take over management of the shop and turn it around. He had heard of my success from several sales reps. This was because I always made time to talk to salespeople and how Mr. Payne had heard about how I resurrected Dutchie's.

Mr. Payne set up an interview with me. I went, liked

what I saw, and knew I was up to the challenge. I promised that as the new manager I would put Braho's in the black, even if I had to cut my own salary to do it. Now I had to tackle the only problem in the whole arrangement: telling Connie that our honeymoon would have to be delayed again. I hated to disappoint her.

I should have known by now how Connie would react. She was disappointed, but she knew of my ambitions and supported my decision. Since I had no formal education she knew the only way for us to succeed was to have our own business. She wanted that for me and realized that this would be an important stepping stone to that end.

We moved to an apartment in Hammond near Braho's while mother found an apartment in a Polish neighborhood in Chicago. I was able to run the Braho's as if it were my own. On Sundays when it was closed I did electrical work. I also replaced eighty percent of the employees. Those remaining did not like the changes I was making. Each change was a struggle. Some of the waitresses had their own "enterprises," giving away free coffee and desserts in return for bigger tips. I even hired a chef who had a bigger salary than mine. I ran a tight ship and soon, as I had promised Mr. Payne, the business was in the black. Connie quit her IIT position and took a job at Braho's as a cashier. We were back working together as usual.

The clientele of Braho's included many businesspeople and I listened to their conversations in hopes of gaining some snippets of information. One of the customers was Libby Posner who owned her own real estate business. Ms. Posner was listing an older two-family house that was a real "fixer-upper" in a nice neighborhood for $16,000. She mentioned it to me and said if I were interested she would guide me through the transaction. With $2,000 of my own money for a down payment, the bank was willing to loan me $11,000. I still needed $3,000 more, so I approached the two

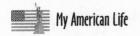 

sisters who were selling the home and made a private contract with them to pay the $3,000 in monthly installments over the next two years.

I was quite happy. With only $2,000 I had purchased a $16,000 home. It was another invaluable lesson on how to manipulate money through private deals; something else to broaden my education.

We had been paying $125 per month plus utilities for our one bedroom apartment. Our new two-family house had a three-room apartment that I rented out for $75.00 per month which I used to pay off the private loan. I took the $125 per month we had been paying in rent and used it to make the mortgage payments. Once the private loan had been repaid, I began making double mortgage payments and in five years the house was paid off. We remodeled the kitchen and bathroom and installed new aluminum siding. One of the additional benefits was in taxes—fifty percent of the improvements I'd made to the income property were tax deductible.

I knew I never would have done as well had I stayed in the old Polish neighborhood. I had gotten where I was by learning from the people I had worked for; they were my real teachers. Now, too, I had a better command of the English language and I read two or three newspapers a day and many business magazines in hopes of learning as much as I could.

On April 12, 1959, Connie gave birth to our son, Arthur, Jr. She quit Braho's in order to stay home with the little one. When I had some quiet moments I would think back to those days in Russia and Germany, and think of how much better off I was now. I had a loving wife, a new son, a home, a satisfying job and many new American friends in addition to those from the old world. I felt truly blessed. The days in the old country seemed like another life, almost one that had been lived by somebody else.

During my two years at Braho's I never got a raise.

What I did get from working with the chef, though, was knowledge about different cuts of meat and how to work with a full menu rather than fast foods. I had not been familiar with food descriptions such as "chicken a la king" or "salisbury steak," but the chef never knew. Each time I heard him mention a new dish I would head for the cookbooks and look it up.

Running a restaurant, I feel, is good experience for running any type of business. If you can be successful in the highly competitive world of food service and not become a statistic in the high rate of failure, you can be a successful business owner. In the restaurant business you take raw material; you must know how to prepare it correctly, and you or your employees have to know how to serve it to customers to their satisfaction. A clean and attractive atmosphere is imperative.

Even though I was content for the time being with my position at Braho's, I applied to manage a new Howard Johnson's in north Hammond. I was hired. My immediate supervisor was a very sharp woman for whom I enjoyed working. The company gave most of their managers Tuesdays off, but would have them come in for a three or four hour meeting. I didn't mind, though. I looked at it as another portion of my education. And the company was pleased with me because I had increased their net profits.

Some of the women who worked at Braho's tried to follow me to Howard Johnson's but I couldn't hire them. It was against my principles—I felt it was stealing from my former employer. When they came in to apply, I told them I just couldn't do it.

There was one exception; her name was Vivian. I had turned her away some weeks earlier and now she was back. But she had quit her job at Braho's two weeks earlier and she needed work. She, her two sisters, mother and brother had all worked for me at one time or another. Considering the fact that she wasn't at Braho's currently, I hired her.

The grand opening of the Howard Johnson's took place with a ceremony and Hammond Mayor Dowling and me cutting the ribbon. I was very proud again and thought what a good idea it had been for me to move away from the Polish neighborhood in Chicago. My advice to any immigrant who would ask would be this: to live in the United States and be successful, you must become more American and less of your nationality. If America is to be your new home, you should be loyal to it.

March 3, 1961, brought us our second baby, Lisa Ann. Arthur Jr. was now a busy two-year-old. Neither he nor his new sister kept us awake nights.

On my way down Calumet Avenue to and from Howard Johnson's I would pass a vacant Burger Chef building. It seemed there were always cars of people pulling into the parking lot to see if it was open. One day I left home a little early and pulled into the lot myself and sat for awhile. Several cars drove in and when the drivers saw the restaurant was closed, drove away. I got out of my car and walked around the building, then peeked inside. The building was totally empty except for two wooden picnic tables. While I was standing there, another car pulled in the lot and stopped near me. The driver rolled down his window.

"Is this place opened?" he asked.

"Not yet, but it soon will be," I answered.

As soon as I said those words, I knew I was going to make my dream come true for our family. I'd been in the United States for seven years and I knew I was ready.

When I got home I told Connie my thoughts for the undertaking. She said we might as well do it because it couldn't involve any more effort than I was already putting out for someone else. The profits might as well go in our pockets. She was ready to work with me again and supported me wholeheartedly in this new venture.

I did some preliminary figuring and calculated we'd need $6,000 to purchase $35,000 worth of used equipment. Unfortunately, we didn't have that much, so I decided to see if I could borrow it. I visited several of my suppliers and asked each for $1,000 to help get me started. They were aware of my success with Braho's Coffee Shop and Howard Johnson's, so they obliged. I was truly gratified with their confidence in me. Many of those people had once been in my position. One, Mr. Zola, a cigarette and tobacco goods vendor, told me that he had failed many times in business before he was successful. He never even asked me to sign a promissory note and told me, "If you don't make it, don't worry about paying me back."

For the rest of my career as a restaurateur, I was faithful to these people who had loaned me the money to get started. They were paid back not only with dollars, but also with my loyalty. Out of respect for the trust Mr. Zola had in me, he was the first one repaid.

There was one other person I had asked for a loan; Uncle Cass and—surprise—he never got back to me. It was the last time I ever asked him for a favor.

While I was still working for Howard Johnson's I began purchasing equipment, mostly used, for the building. The building and the Burger Chef property had been owned by Eugene Specker who had donated it to Calumet College, but continued to manage it for them. I leased it for $500 a month for five years.

I had given my notice to the management at Howard Johnson's, but they asked me if I would stay on until a suitable replacement could be found. I agreed. They were very accommodating and even let me go to their warehouse to pick out equipment I could use which they would then sell to me at a fair price. The malt machine I found there served me for eighteen years.

Mr. Barrett, the general manager of Howard Johnson's,

had been grooming me to supervise all of the Howard Johnson's in the state of Ohio. He told me that if I ever failed as a business owner, I was welcome to return to the company at any time and that Howard Johnson's legal department would help me get out of my lease.

It was nerve-wracking to go $6,000 into debt. With two small children, Connie and I had a full load. We figured we would both have to find other jobs to pay back the debt if the business went under. My greatest help in this new business came from Connie who agreed to don a car hop uniform with the rest of our crew. With her experience at Richards, Dutchie's and Braho's she was my "Girl Friday" as well as loving wife and mother to the children.

Art's Drive-In opened on June 15, 1961. The place looked beautiful. All of the carhops were dressed in first class uniforms. Vividly hued flowers flowed from boxes which bordered the building on the Calumet Avenue side with more of the same bordering the lot along the south side. The gardens were a mainstay of Art's from spring through fall for the next eighteen years, a tradition I that had begun many years ago in

*Where it all began—Art's Drive-In on Calumet Avenue in Hammond, Indiana.*

Scotland at the Polish Veterans Club.

The first day's receipts were $150. We were thrilled, since I figured that $100 was the break-even point.

*Art and a young helper hard at work at the grill of the drive-in.*

During the lunch rush hour Connie hired a babysitter so she could be at the restaurant to help serve the students from two nearby high schools. She'd come back later in the evening to close the restaurant. I would be there at 10:00 a.m. and would work until 10:00 p.m. The restaurant hours were from 10:00 a.m. to 1:00 a.m. weekdays and 10:00 a.m. until 2:00 a.m. weekends. Many times people scheduled to work would not show up for one reason or another and Connie and I would have to fill in. There were nights when either one or sometimes both of us were almost too exhausted to sleep.

I've always believed in sharing some of my good fortune with the community; "Never take more than you give," as Elton John expounded. Whatever you share comes back to you in greater amounts. It was our policy at Art's to give a free hamburger for each "A" a student received on his or her report card. This brought in swarms of students. The children were honest and the promotion was a success. Only once did a student manage to get a hamburger after doing a little forgery on his report card. Over the years we had "free ice cream for everyone" promotions and prizes such as radios and watches for the best Halloween costume. Sometimes we would hire bands and close off a portion of the parking lot for dancing.

One time a former Hammond High student who was serving in Vietnam had a letter printed in the Hammond Times' *Voice of the People* section. In it he stated that what he missed about home was Art's great hamburgers. For the first month after he returned home, that soldier received all the

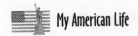 

Sunday, June 13, 1971

*Viet vet George Pinkerton's hamburger dream comes true.*

## Platter Pile of 'Burgers Fills Serviceman's Dream

free hamburgers from Art's he could eat.

Linda Tolle, another young customer who lived nearby, would come into Art's every lunch hour during the school year simply to listen to the jukebox. She was using her lunch money for music—something which, as a teenager, meant more to her than food. When I found out, I made her buy a hamburger with her money, put change from the register in the jukebox and let her make her selections.

On June 3, 1963, we were blessed with a third child, John. Our restaurant business was in full swing and, hectic though it was, things settled into a routine. I began dabbling in the stock market and during slow periods had some time to improve my chess playing ability. George Chalos, a customer, saw my chess board set up and asked if he might challenge me to a game. We played in the back while we watched stock market reports zip past on the screen of the small television I had installed for just that purpose. George took me to his chess club in Hammond, which I eventually joined. My playing improved to a point where I defeated a master in a tournament—not once but twice.

*Art and his good friend George Chalos enjoying a game of chess in the back of Art's Drive-In.*

# Chapter 18
# Going Home

*"There is no delight in owning
anything unshared."*

*—Seneca*

Mother was finally able to return to Poland in 1965 to
see members or her family that she hadn't seen in fifty-three

*The Lukowski family in 1965
(From left to right) Arthur, Jr., Connie, Lisa,
Josephine and John*

years; the family that she had been whisked past as she rode with me in the cattle car of a German train. She was very happy to have had the opportunity to see her sisters and brothers, but melancholy over the fact that she couldn't see Anatole and Zan; the travel agency informed her that she would be unable to enter the Soviet Union to visit them. She asked that Connie and I travel with her to Poland the following year.

The trip never materialized. Mother died of a heart attack on March 9, 1966. What was heartbreaking to me was what I learned later—that tourists had been going to the U.S.S.R. prior to 1965 and the travel agent had misinformed mother. She missed fulfilling her dream of more than twenty years because of an incorrect piece of information. From this I learned that if you are in a situation requiring your action where someone or something means a great deal to you, do not rely on the word of another as to how you should proceed; check out everything for yourself.

When Zan learned that mother had died, he almost had a nervous breakdown. In letters his wife, Nadia, told me that Zan took out photographs of his mother and spoke to them. He had even gotten to the point where he would go to the window to see if mother was coming down the street toward the house. She asked if I could please come to Kiev.

Nadia's plea resulted in me making the first more than twenty trips I would eventually make to Kiev. When I got there I found that conditions had improved only slightly since before World War II. Housing was in such short supply that eight people sharing two rooms was the norm.

Anatole was working as a truck driver and this was the case for him and his family. Besides having four generations of family members that included Hala and himself, Hala's mother, Anatole's daughter, Johna, her husband, Victor, their daughter, Tanya, in his assigned two rooms, they had to share a kitchen and bathroom with three other families.

The cramped kitchen contained a sink, a table, and a four-burner stove which each family used according to a schedule. The bathroom was the size of a closet and held contained only a toilet. Each family kept its own toilet seat for cleanliness and a sense of privacy. The rooms of the apartment were so small that Anatole slept on a day bed on the balcony of the apartment whenever the weather permitted.

Zan and his family, in comparison, lived in absolute luxury by Soviet standards. He had become a Communist Party member which entitled him to a better apartment and job—as Assistant to the Ministry of Agriculture of the Ukraine. Zan and Nadia, their boys Valerie and Henry, and daughter, Anna, had a three-room apartment with its own kitchen and bath.

While I was visiting, I bought each of the families a new refrigerator made in Poland. Neither Hala nor Nadia had ever had the luxury of a refrigerator before. During sightseeing trips in Kiev I took pictures with my Polaroid camera. This never failed to attract the curious who had never seen instant pictures before.

I found Anatole to be quite open about the situation in his country while Zan was afraid to discuss many subjects. He was privy to knowledge of the government's capabilities and was certain that we were being watched since I was an American visitor. A single letter sent from Scotland by mother and me requesting information of Zan's whereabouts resulted in the loss of his party membership and his job for a year. It seems that party members were required to declare if they had relatives in the West. As far as Zan knew, he didn't have any. He was forced to get many signatures on a petition stating that he had no knowledge that his mother and brother were still alive. The process of gathering signatures and having the government grant approval for reinstatement took a year.

I also learned that Vala, my almost-first date, was working for post office security, but I dared not contact her for fear of the same thing happening to her—or something even worse.

When I finally had a chance to have a heart-to-heart talk with my brothers, I was able to assure them that mother had a good life in the United States and had been happy there. By the conclusion of my visit the spirits of both brothers were lifted and Zan was out of his depressed state.

Three years passed before I returned to Kiev. This time, it was with the whole family. Art, Jr. was ten, Lisa was eight, and John was six.

When we entered the U.S.S.R., every courtesy available was extended to us. I can only surmise that it was so the government could impress Connie and the children with the benefits of communism. It was rare opportunity indeed to have an American family with young children as tourists behind the Iron Curtain in those days. We were given two interpreters, a driver and a "Chijka" (a government limousine complete with Soviet flags) at our disposal for many hours each day. As accommodations we were given a two-bedroom hotel suite in Kiev. This was done for two reasons: first, Soviet relatives had no extra space; secondly, it was easier for the government to keep tabs on foreigners.

And keep tabs on us they did. When I went to the hotel clerk to order the limousine for the evening I found that it had already been arranged. Rules were bent at the restaurants we visited. Normally children weren't allowed in after 7:00 pm, but we could dine as a family at any hour.

Connie was aware that hotel maids had gone through the suitcases. Nothing was taken; they were merely curious. After a day out in the city, Connie understood their interest.

In the hotel restaurant, she learned to ask the waiter what was available instead of ordering what was on the menu. When Connie decided to have her hair done in the hotel's beauty shop, she had to run back up the stairs to our room to grab her shampoo since none was provided for customers. The stairs were preferable to the elevators which frequently stalled between floors. When we walked the streets of Kiev or rode the metro, some people would smile at us. Others would take a second look, or even follow us for awhile. Women would sometimes gently touch the fabric of Connie's dress or coat.

And then there were the lines—long lines that stretched down the streets from every shop. It was almost painful to see them. Connie wondered how anyone ever had time to fix meals with so much time spent in lines waiting to buy food. It brought back to me the memories of my trips to the government store with mother. Outside the city many villages still had community wells and straw houses with thatched roofs, just as they had when I was a boy.

"Living itself is a chore in the U.S.S.R.," Connie told me. She was quite accurate.

The highlight of our trip was becoming acquainted and reacquainted with my family. My Soviet relatives were warm and friendly. They prepared meals for us and took us sightseeing.

During our visit American astronauts Neil Armstrong and Edwin Aldrin, Jr., walked on the moon. When we came down to breakfast we found an American flag on our table out of respect for that great achievement of the United States. Ironically, but not surprisingly to me, a huge front page spread in the Soviet newspaper captured the details of Ted Kennedy's unfortunate car accident at Martha's Vineyard which resulted in the drowning death Mary Jo Kopechne. Details of the moon landing were relegated to a tiny article on page five.

# Chapter 19

# Enjoying Success

*"In this world it is not what we take up, but what we give up that makes us rich."*

—*Henry Ward Beecher*

Louis Schilling was a rare man—an oxymoron—an architect who loved nature. It was not unusual to find an odd curve in a driveway or a sidewalk at an unusual angle, done so as to not destroy a tree on the grounds of a house he designed and built. Connie and I saw one of his houses in Dyer, Indiana as he was preparing it for an open house. We liked it and, after thinking it over for two days, decided to purchase it for his asking price. I told Louis that since we didn't haggle over his asking price, that he should agree to my terms as to how I wanted to pay for the house. I offered to give him $25,000 down and pay the rest in $5,000 increments every six months with no interest. Louis discussed the matter with his wife and his attorney, and agreed to do it. We shook hands. In August of 1969 after our return from the Ukraine, we settled into our new residence.

The ensuing years were prosperous. As always, I listened to the sales reps who sold me their products for Art's Drive-In. I must admit I was filled with pride and a sense of accomplishment when I learned that I was selling more french fries, buns, and fountain drinks than either the McDonald's or Burger King down the road.

Art, Jr. and Lisa worked at the drive-in during their summer vacations and on weekends. The summer that Art, Jr. was fourteen he rode his bicycle to the drive-in, worked eight hours, then peddled back home—a distance of fourteen miles. John, who had been in charge of driving the John Deere tractor and mowing the grass at home since he was eight, went on to do weeding and outside work at the drive-in as well. At fourteen, Lisa began her employment at Art's.

The children attended Morgan Park Academy, twenty-six miles from home, and sacrificed much of their social lives because of the distance and the obligation they felt to the business.

In 1977 Zan was finally given permission to visit the U.S. He had been filling out forms and applications for ten years. New requests were required each year and nine had been denied. The Soviets only allowed 600 people per year to visit western countries. Zan was granted permission for a three month visit.

Poor Zan never relaxed while he was here. He assumed that every place—our house, the drive-in, our automobiles—was bugged. The timing of the visit was fortunate for Zan was able to attend both John's eighth grade graduation and Art, Jr.'s high school graduation.

During his visit one Saturday night there was a grease fire in the grill at the drive-in. The fire department arrived and quickly extinguished it, but the fire had burned a six foot hole through the ceiling.

"You'll probably be closed for a month," one of the firemen said as he was cleaning up to leave.

The next morning, Sunday, at 5:00 a.m. I began calling my tradesmen friends. A master carpenter, George King, and another electrician friend spent all of Sunday at the drive-in along with my thirty-seven member crew. Everything was repaired and cleaned by that evening.

Monday the fire chief stopped by.

"I'm here to assess the damage the Saturday night fire did to your building," he told me.

"What fire?" I asked with a bemused look on my face.

Zan was amazed at my ingenuity and proud of my success. He was intrigued by all our "luxuries" such as a garbage disposal, remote control television, and automatic garage door opener.

When he was ready to leave, we loaded him down with parcels. Since he was traveling by ship from New York Harbor, there were no baggage limits as there were on airplanes. Zan wept as he got ready to depart.

"Brother, you live in a different world," he said tearfully.

When he arrived in the Ukraine with so many packages, some of the items were confiscated. He wouldn't discuss the particulars, so we never learned which items he was allowed to keep.

Art, Jr. attended Wabash College to major in science. Lisa attended Purdue University Calumet while working full time for the Lake County Prosecutor's Office. John graduated from Hanover College in southern Indiana.

With a sense of nostalgia, I leased the old Richard's Drive-In on Stoney Island where Connie and I had met in 1955. I took a partner in this new venture because I didn't want it to divert my attention from the operation of Art's. My partner also had another business interest as well. Before long it was evident that Richard's was not being managed to my standards and I chose not to renew the lease.

There comes a time when, after pouring heart and soul into a project, one experiences a burnout period. The late 1970s were that period for me. The combination of my desire for a new dissimilar enterprise and the fact that more

and more fast food businesses were coming into the area convinced me that it was time to sell.

In 1979, I sold Art's Drive-In and was unemployed for
the first time since I was a boy.

# Chapter 20
# Starting Over

*"Few of us can stand prosperity—
another man's, I mean."*

—*Mark Twain*

For some months in 1980, Connie and I shopped for a business. We would travel around, always on the lookout for new opportunities. Although my mind was completely open to new business ideas, I seemed to gravitate back to the food service industry.

I still read three or four newspapers daily, but I was partial to the *Wall Street Journal*. Much of my success in the stock market was due to business information I found within its articles. After setting aside the Journal I was going over the Hammond Times and saw an article which mentioned an upcoming public seminar by Franchise Concepts. The company had information on many new businesses and would look for possible financing for entrepreneurs.

Since I was really seeking an opportunity outside of the food industry, I picked up many different brochures. I had a friend in the auto industry who was interested in the food industry, so I picked up some brochures for him, too. By the time I left I had information on just about every type of business in the country.

One brochure covered the new fast lube business. There weren't any in the area, the closest being in New York and Salt Lake City. I took all the information I had, sharpened my pencil, and began figuring.

My friend Harry saw my preliminary figures and was impressed enough to volunteer his help to do further research into the fast lube industry. He visited the New York location, then the two of us spent several days visiting fourteen different lube shops in Salt Lake City.

We saw some things we liked and some things we didn't like in the way the garages operated. We considered purchasing a franchise, but decided Utah was too far away for a franchisor to give us as much help as we might need. One operator offered to sell us blueprints for $3,500; but after discussing the plans with an architect, we discovered that it would cost the same with or without them in order to build to the State of Indiana's specifications.

At this time the construction business in Indiana was poor, with area companies going broke. Unemployment in the area was at 17% and people were leaving the area. The steel mills in northwest Indiana were laying off people at all levels as they downsized and became more automated.

Over the next six months I had more than two hundred meetings with realtors, bankers, builders, suppliers, architects, oil company executives, equipment reps; even coffee machine distributors, ad agencies and on and on.

Harry was in the process of selling his car care business while operating an ice cream shop at a local mall. I spent my time scouting locations and checking out contractors. When the two of us would get together, we'd share information and rate it on a scale of one to ten to find the best choices. We agreed on a location on Route 41 in Highland, Indiana, for our shop. We negotiated a price, made a down payment, and bought the land on contract.

What came next turned out to be the most difficult

part of the venture: getting the business financed. We had expected a bit of difficulty, but not the number of stone walls we encountered.

One of the first banks we tried suggested we remodel an old gas station to prove that a lube center could be successful since there were none in the area that the bank could inspect before granting us approval. I rejected this idea because I wanted to start with a clean, modern building specifically designed for our purpose. We kept looking.

I took Connie with me on one of my outings so she would have an opportunity to see what we were up against. We went to our bank where we had been loyal customers since 1958 when we first moved to Hammond. I set up a business account there when I managed Braho's Coffee Shop and opened a personal account there. I did the same with Art's Drive In. As collateral, we still owned the Art's Drive In property and our home in Dyer. We were debt-free. The bank management was aware of my talent for growing and improving businesses.

All Connie and I needed was $140,000 but the bank wanted $450,000 in collateral—literally everything we owned. We brought this information to our attorney who confirmed what we already knew—400 % collateral was absurd and such a bad deal that we shouldn't even consider it. We returned to the bank to meet the loan officer.

"Our attorney told us the amount of collateral was ridiculous and the deal is so bad we shouldn't seriously consider it," Connie told him.

"Then I suggest you borrow the money from your attorney," the officer replied smugly, "since he obviously knows what's best."

I could see the blood rising up Connie's neck and into her face. She leaned forward and replied in a very controlled manner. "That's exactly what I would do if I had been depositing my money with my lawyer for the last twenty years!" We

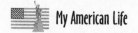 

got up and walked out.

When we returned home there was an apology from the banker on our answering machine. But it was too little too late. It saddened me to realize how some lending institutions operate. Even though they have profited largely by using your money for many years and know you have an excellent track record, they have no loyalty and act as if they owe you nothing. These bankers didn't even consider the jobs we would be bringing to the community they serve and with them, new accounts. Connie and I might as well have been strangers walking through their doors for the first time. Even then, we wouldn't have deserved the treatment we got.

We had no choice but to sell the stocks we had accumulated over the years. This was a period of recession and we sold them at a fifty percent loss. Over the years we'd picked out silver coins that passed through the cash register and had collected them in a gallon jug, which was now full. To our astonishment, the coins were worth $38,000. Harry sold his business and took out a second and third mortgage on his home.

When the construction began, I insisted that the office be located in such a way that the technicians working on the floor could be viewed from inside. It was my policy in all of my businesses: Watch the work being done. I also insisted on white cement from Canada which cost $3,000 more. When I requested that the walls be snow white, the architect objected because he felt it wasn't practical. I told him I wanted the shop to be as clean as a dentist's office. During our research period I discovered that most of the family cars were brought in by women. I wanted to impress them with a sparkling clean establishment.

To be certain that motor homes could be serviced I had some friends, Dean and Pat Conner, bring theirs in to measure the height and width for a special oversized door. We also had the basement dug ten inches deeper than necessary so, in the event that the quick lube business failed, the building would be more easily adapted for another type of business use.

When it was finally time to paint that winter we were short of cash so Harry and I did it ourselves. I had to wear a snowmobile suit to keep from freezing.

For proper drainage, the foundation of the building was two inches higher than the pavement of State Highway 41. Because of this the highway department required the installation of a sewer—at our expense— from Route 41 back to Spring Street, 800 feet away. The cheapest estimate we obtained for the sewer installation was $45,000 which we didn't have. I knew we would have to do it ourselves. I hired Don Krawczyk to dig the trenches. Don let Art, Jr. use his surveying equipment and the three of us put in the sewer tiles and manhole covers.

In some places the trench was seven feet deep. We encountered many old irrigation tiles that spilled water into our trenches and had to be pumped out. The whole affair was dirty, backbreaking labor. When my son and I came home each night we would shed our dirty clothes directly into the garbage, clean up, eat dinner and go straight to bed. We worked for a week from 7:00 am to 7:00 pm. Connie would bring us lunch to minimize the amount of time we'd be out of the trenches.

In the end the job cost us $16,000. We saved $29,000. For me, the whole project was all too reminiscent of my slave labor days in the German camp.

Now that the building was completed, we were still in need of $44,000 to get the business off the ground. We had no choice but to borrow this amount at twenty-two percent interest. Since Harry was already mortgaged to the limit, I had to take on the loan myself. Connie only had $13.00 left in the checking account. We lived off of food we had in our freezer and bought as little as possible. My friend George Chalos came by for chess one evening while Connie and I were laughing at our situation. He felt so sorry for us that he reached into his wallet and handed Connie ten one-hundred dollar bills.

"Just pay me back whenever you can. I'm not worried," he told her.

On March 6, 1980, Connie's birthday, Oil Express was born. I had sent out more than one hundred notices to friends and former colleagues to let them know about the new enterprise. That first day Oil Express serviced seventeen cars. The notices did their job because the first week seventy-five of the cars we serviced belonged to my friends who were there because of the notices. The support and encouragement from my friends gave me confidence that our business would succeed. It made the many sleepless nights Connie and I had all worthwhile. We had twenty-four years worth of work on the line.

"But if we lose, we'll begin again," said Connie. She remembered that Mr. Zola had begun several businesses before he was successful. Even more, she trusted me for having done my homework.

The day of the grand opening Connie's sister, Mary, had come out with her son, John Holloway, to celebrate with us. They expected to walk into a restaurant. What a surprise they had when they discovered the grand opening was for a quick lube shop! John was immensely impressed; he had always appreciated my business acumen.

John introduced me to his friend, a former governor of Illinois, Dan Walker. The two of them were interested in going into some kind of business together as well. As a former governor, Dan was well-known and supposedly well-connected. He felt he could open doors for the growth of Oil Express by getting investors.

After three months of discussions, Harry and I agreed to let John and Dan become involved in Oil Express. I had been busy checking out possible locations for new stores when I wasn't managing the first one in Highland. When I found a suitable location I'd go to meetings of the city zoning board. It was an almost non-stop schedule.

We had an agreement that John and Dan could open ten Oil Express stores in the Chicago area. In order to generate income for themselves five would be their own and five would be franchised, with Harry and I receiving $5,000 for each store. In return for the five privately-owned stores, Dan would draw up the documents necessary for us to be able to sell additional franchises. It seemed a very fair arrangement. Before Dan and John were able to borrow money from banks, I had to provide a track record of growth for the Highland store and guarantee the loans. They were able to obtain a loan from the Small Business Administration through the South Shore Bank in south Chicago.

I was anxious to begin franchising, confident that the public was ready for our services. I was keenly aware that we needed assistance in legal matters and wanted Dan to handle that portion of the operation. John would be trained to be the "hands on" person, much like myself.

At one point during the first year of operation, Harry's best friend showed an interest in getting in on the ground floor of Oil Express. We wanted the business to grow and thrive, so we began putting a store together for him. Dan Walker worked on the franchising documents. A contractor, George Karras, was willing to build a shop in north Hammond and would lease it to Oil Express to use either as a company-owned shop or for a franchisee. He had full confidence in the business and felt there would be no risk either way. We had several other people interested in purchasing a franchise, but first consideration was to go to Harry's friend.

As the construction of the building neared completion and it was almost time to have Harry's friend sign the lease, Harry began to hedge a bit, suggesting that perhaps they consider selling the franchise to someone else.

"Harry, we promised this franchise to your friend. We gave him our word," I reminded him.

"Screw friends. This is business," he replied.

I held firm. I also began to worry.

Harry had become increasingly difficult to work with. He was always changing the work schedule. Sometimes he wanted to work three days a week, then he'd change his mind and want to work every other week. Sometimes he'd express a desire to franchise our five shops and other times he preferred that we keep the shops in partnership. He no longer wanted to take any business calls at home, so all after hours calls were directed to me.

Dan Walker's wife Roberta was a beautiful, talented and clever woman determined to be involved in the lube business in a big way. I started training her at the Highland store to work downstairs underneath the cars and upstairs under the hood. We spent hours in the office where I taught her how to hire technicians and train them, how to relate to customers, the importance of advertising, and so on. She came away with a notebook full of information. Connie took Roberta to lunch several times a week to give her a break from the training sessions. John Holloway received the same training. This irritated Harry. He disliked the inconvenience of them being trained in the shop, but it was the only practical way to do it.

The relationship between Harry and me was deteriorating. Newspaper articles about the business did not always mention Harry, and there he had a legitimate complaint. Everyone knew I had a partner, but generally I was the one being interviewed so I was the one who was mentioned. Many stories had been written in the past about Art's Drive In and readers were curious about my new enterprise. I desperately wanted the Hammond Oil Express to succeed. I was well known in the neighborhood not only for the drive in but also as manager of Braho's Coffee Shop and the north Hammond Howard Johnson's Restaurant.

One morning as the construction of the north Hammond building was in its final stages, I received a call from George Karras. He said I needed to come to the site because of a big problem.

When I arrived he told me that one of his workers had called my partner Harry about 6:00 am to get some information about a construction detail.

"Call Art. I'm washing my hands of the whole project," he told the worker.

It seems he had again changed his mind about franchising. He said I was welcome to keep the unit or franchise it—either way, he wanted out. He was tired of dealing with so many people. One of my strong points was having the temperament to deal with various types of people. Harry, although quite intelligent and talented in business, found that type of networking distasteful. He suggested that he take over full management of the Highland store for a salary. We'd split the profits and he would train the crew for the new north Hammond store. I agreed.

With Harry out of the picture as far as franchising, I realized that I could use help finding locations, meeting bankers, interviewing potential franchisees among other things. There was a lot of money to be made in quick lube franchising. I was also aware that in order to advertise successfully, I needed more than a couple of stores—a lesson I learned when McDonald's and Burger King moved into the area near Art's Drive In. A small operator cannot afford to buy TV advertising. I wanted to grow rapidly. Dan and John thought they were up to the task, so the three of us formed what was known as Oil Express National. I retained fifty-one percent of the stock, while Dan and John split the remaining forty-nine percent equally. This allowed me to maintain controlling stock in the company, something which I always recommend.

At this time—August, 1980—the Hammond Oil Express opened for business. People in the neighborhood were excited that I was back. Many had been former customers; some had even been my employees. They proved to be loyal new customers as well.

The franchisee's brother, Ron, was an extremely capable business man. He and I visited most of the businesses in north Hammond and East Chicago. We went to Gavit High School to have hundreds of discount coupons printed up and distributed them. Walter and Mary Kasprzycki, owners of a Polish-American restaurant named the Cavalier Inn passed out literally hundreds. We made up placards and put them on utility poles all the while hoping that the Northern Indiana Public Service Company (NIPSCO) would not be too eager to take them down. At the end of the first month we averaged forty cars daily. In three months there wasn't one day when I didn't spend some time in the shop. Actually I put in more hours that first year than the franchisee himself.

The average family income in north Hammond in 1980 was between $15,000 and $18,000. These folks were not driving a new car every year and were pleased to have a place to take their cars for convenient, affordable service—an alternative to dealerships and garages.

I ran into a friend one day who informed me that Oil Express had been written up in *Inc. Magazine*. This came as a complete surprise to me, so I went and purchased a copy. I flipped through the pages looking for the article and stopped abruptly when I came across a picture of two familiar figures. There were Dan Walker and John Holloway standing inside the Highland Oil Express. The article went on to explain how the two of them were bringing the Oil Express ten minute lube system to the Chicago area. There was not a word about Harry or me.

I went to John for an explanation.

"The reporter called very early in the morning. I thought it was too early in the morning to bother you," he told me.

That's odd, I thought. It wasn't too early to get Dan to drive in from Oak Brook. It wasn't too early for John to drive in from Chicago. It was, however, apparently too early for me to drive ten minutes from my home in Dyer.

Shortly after this we had a meeting scheduled at a bank in Chicago to discuss Oil Express National business. When I arrived I was ushered into one conference room while Dan and John were seated in another. I was puzzled.

A banker entered with a proposal which he handed to me. It had been devised by John and Dan. They wanted me to surrender fourteen percent of my Oil Express National Stock for the sum of $500,000. This would leave me with thirty-seven percent instead of fifty-one percent and effectively take away my control of the company.

I wasn't even tempted. After all my years of painstaking labor in the restaurant business, all the sleepless nights Connie and I spent worrying about how to raise capital, worrying about bank loans, our risks, sacrifices—I'd be damned if I'd give up the lion's share of the business to two people who just stepped in—not after all we'd been through. Besides, I

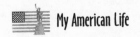 

wondered, where would they come up with the $500,000?

Two hours into the "meeting" I found out. They planned to borrow it from banks using Oil Express as collateral. Now I saw why they were in a separate room—they didn't have the guts to face me. The banker shuttling back and forth seemed ashamed for the way Dan and John were operating. Although he was there for money, too, I could sense that this was not a day's work of which he was proud.

In a nutshell, John and Dan planned to raise money on my company, then use that money to take control of the company away from me, leaving me a junior partner. And the bank knew, from my financial statements and the increase in the number of cars in our shops, that there was enough potential to loan Dan and John the money. A sweet deal. What a shame, I thought, that all the energy they had put in to this proposal hadn't been directed toward the development of Illinois Oil Express. I was now aware that I needed at least partial omnipotence when it came to dealing with my partners.

Connie hated the way I had to deal with the Walkers from that point on. They needed insurance; they had to have an income of $50,000 a year and all this while the Illinois Oil Express was not generating a positive cash flow. Where was all this money supposed to come from? Their demands kept coming but I refused to give in to them.

The son of Dan's lawyer had offices in Oak Brook and would sometimes let his father use the conference rooms for meetings. During a break at one of these meetings, a colleague of Dan's came up to me with an envelope. He put a finger to his lips to let me know this was to be kept secret. I slipped the envelope into my pocket until after the meeting when I opened it in my car. Inside was a copy of a letter from Dan to Mr. Butler of Butler Aviation in which he stated that he and his wife had learned the fast lube business from me. He went on to say that although I was a really great guy and a Christian fellow and that they had nothing in the world against me, he and Roberta felt that they had secured enough knowledge to run a chain of shops without me. At last Dan had apparently found a backer.

When Dan made his break from the company, he intended to turn his shares of the Illinois Oil Express and the National Oil Express over to John Holloway. I promised him a lawsuit and a great deal of publicity if he attempted to do. Everyone involved was aware that Dan was setting up a separate, competing corporation with Butler while still an Oil Express partner—and behind the back of his current partner.

Dan turned over his shares of Oil Express in exchange for the letter that had been secretly given to me. I still look on the entire episode disdainfully. If the Walkers, Butler, Holloway, and the Lukowskis could have worked together, we could have built and managed several hundred fast lube shops. At the time oil companies were being given tremendous assistance—they were the business trend of the 1980s. I was certainly willing to share in partnership but I was not willing to allow Machiavellianism to embitter me and spoil a business that had thrived on honesty.

While all this was taking place, Illinois Oil Express was building a shop in Bridgeview that was to be for John and Dan. It became solely John's.

John and Dan had completed development of the franchise agreement with which I sold franchises, so I didn't feel my year of dealing with Dan Walker was a total waste. Still, the day Dan left was a joyous one for Connie. She knew how strain-filled my dealings with him were. And the end was complete in every sense of the word. At conventions, the Walkers would not even acknowledge us. Connie and I got a chuckle when we remembered the $300 bottles of wine with dinner, the chauffeured limousines, and the expensive business luncheons, hallmarks of the Walkers.

The new team of Butler and Walker built thirty-six fast lubes in Chicagoland using the name "B W Oil Change."

Financing was difficult for me and I only had eight slow-growing outlets. But Oil Express became the "Cadillac" of the industry, maintaining higher car counts than any other company of its sort in the United States. The flagship shop in Highland, Indiana, is still one of the three busiest ten minute oil change shops in the country.

Within a few years problems cropped up for BW Oil Change. The Walkers had founded the American Savings and Loan and, as rumor had it, ran into legal trouble when Dan loaned Jiffy Lube money to buy out some of the B W shops. The rumors turned out to be true because that episode landed Dan in prison and begot Roberta a divorce.

In September, 1982, John Holloway was killed in an automobile accident. This left Illinois Oil Express in the hands of John's bank trustees who were counseled by Dan Barnes, John's attorney. The people who had bought three franchises from John broke away from the company and had to be taken to court. Fortunately, Dan Barnes kept excellent records of all meetings involving the sale of franchises. With these records and my testimony and financial help, Oil Express won the suits for John's widow.

I developed a friendship with Dan Barnes during our dealings with the concerns of Illinois Oil Express. Dan was a younger, family man and I felt good in his company. He appreciated my expertise and had come to realize that there was a lot he could learn from me about the fast lube industry.

In Indiana I was putting together two more Oil Express shops for Harry and me. Even though he wanted nothing to do with franchising, he was still interested in private growth. It was at this point Harry offered to buy out my share of the Highland store.

"Gee, I would have offered you $25,000 more than that for your half," I told him.

"It's yours, Art," he replied.

We walked the half a block to the bank to make

arrangements for me to borrow $195,000.

After the financial details were settled, we got back to discussing the two soon-to-be Oil Express shops. One was ready to open in Merrillville, Indiana, and the other in South Holland, Illinois was still in negotiations. Harry chose the Merrillville location.

My two sons and I had already distributed thousands of coupons throughout the Merrillville area. We had even been chased out of a few parking lots while placing them under windshield wipers. Our efforts helped Harry get off to a good start. He kept the name Oil Express for a couple of years to take advantage of the benefits of advertising, but changed it after that. He still has a successful business today. And with the acquisition of the Highland store, my assets reached $1 million.

I continued to scout for new locations and found an available lot in South Holland, Illinois. It was not directly in the business district of the town, so I wasn't really sure if I wanted it or not. It *was* adjacent to a busy railroad track where fifteen to twenty trains passed daily. I had an idea for something I could do when the trains crossed the road and backed up traffic at this location. Plus, I could draw customers from nearby Chicago Heights and Dolton. The more I thought about it, the better I liked it.

I spoke to the owner of the property. He wanted $115,000 for the lot which I thought was very fair since most of my lots had cost around $200,000. Once the owner learned that I might have a problem raising the money since I had already borrowed against my collateral, he decided to sell it for $15,000 with the rest on contract.

I visited the South Holland bank with the owner's proposal, my records of daily car counts from the Highland store, and pictures depicting the beauty and cleanliness of the shop. After a fifteen minute meeting, the banker told me to return in a few days and he might be able to help me.

That weekend it was my turn to manage the Highland store, and it was extremely busy. I didn't pay much attention to a gentleman who entered and began looking around—it was just to hectic. The bays were full and cars awaiting service were lined up outside. During a brief lull, I walked up to the man and asked, "May I help you?" It was only then that I realized that he was the banker from South Holland who had come by to analyze the operation.

The following week I went back to the South Holland banker. He said that if the owner of the property was willing to put the property in trust, the bank would loan me the full amount for the construction of the building. I was tickled. I knew just how to stretch that loan. I had enough money for the first three payments on the loan, to purchase the land for $15,000 down, and $6,000 to invest in an Oil Express sign. There was a $6,000 down payment due on $40,000 worth of equipment but, because of some personal matter concerning the decision of the seller's estate property, it didn't have to be made for another year. What this all amounted to was that I had opened a $650,000 store with a total investment of $27,000.

Prior to the grand opening I mailed 1,000 letters to businesses in the area with six discount coupons for the owners and their employees. I invited them to look us over and enjoy a complimentary cup of coffee and a doughnut.

I also brought to fruition the idea I'd had for the traffic at the railroad crossing while looking the site over. I made a large sign which read, "WHILE WAITING FOR THE TRAIN, COME ON IN FOR A TEN-MINUTE OIL CHANGE." Additionally, I had a technician walk through the stopped traffic handing out discount coupons to the waiting drivers. It was a pleasant surprise to see how many people would hurry in for an oil change while waiting for the gates to go up.

In the first month of operation the South Holland shop averaged fifty cars a day, my break-even point.

# Chapter 21

# The Birthing Pains of Partnerships

*"There is only one success—to be able
to spend your life in your own way."*

—Christopher Morley,
*Where the Blue Begins*

Matchmaking is never simple. It becomes even more difficult when it involves the marriage of partners in a company and the raising of a "family" who will care for their "brainchild." Break-ups are inevitable as was mine with Dan Walker. But I got back up on the horse and began searching for a new mate. Early in 1983 I found Nick, a successful businessman who wanted to purchase ten Oil Express franchises. Nick had made a fortune in building in the Schererville, Indiana, area and owned his own construction company. I was thrilled at the prospect of franchising ten new stores. Nick, his partner, their attorney and I had many lunches and meetings together. Everything went along without a wrinkle. Nick handed me $3,000 in good faith and said he wanted to study the blueprints before signing a franchise agreement.

Six months later I got a call from the man who installed Oil Express equipment for me. It seems when he began installing equipment in a new oil change shop he noticed that the blueprints had the name of Oil Express stamped on them. He didn't wish to be involved in anything

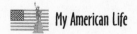 

illegal, so he called to find out what was going on; the business wasn't an Oil Express.

Another incompatible business partner. Nick settled with me before the case went to court. He went on to build many oil change shops and lease them out, but they didn't do well and were subsequently bought up by Jiffy Lube.

Right after the Nick incident I met a man named Dave from Michigan City, Indiana. He owned and operated twenty-one McDonald's franchises with his sons and was always on the lookout for new opportunities for his family. After a succession of meetings together, he thought it would be best if he and I became partners. His idea was to start a new corporation giving me forty percent with he and his sons retaining sixty percent. He also wanted to give me a $50,000 salary, a car, and an office in Michigan City from which to run the operation. I didn't take it. I'd learned to always maintain the controlling interest in my company.

Dave did go on to build six beautiful oil change shops. Unfortunately they were not well run and eventually bought up again by Jiffy Lube. Jiffy Lube was rapidly growing under the masterful command of Jim Hindman from Baltimore, Maryland. Jim, a fantastic businessman, built Jiff Lube into the largest quick lube business in the country.

A Quaker State Oil company executive recommended me to Patricia Tonkovich and Dan Schultz, both of whom were seeking information about the quick lube business. Both currently worked for American Steel Foundries. Pat was a steel buyer, the fourth highest paid executive in the company. After some meetings with me, the two decided to invest in an Oil Express franchise and chose a location in Calumet City. Ironically, my ex-partner and blueprint borrower, Nick, planned to build his own shop just down the road. The race was on!

Just as Pat and Dan's business was ready to open, a funny thing happened—there was no gas or electricity to the building. Requests had been placed with both Northern Illinois and Edison but, mysteriously, both had lost the applications. This meant at least a one month delay in getting hooked up. I had my suspicions that since Nick was a well known builder in the area he probably had some friends in the right places to help the applications turn to vapor. Luckily I had a friend, too—a city attorney who called the public service departments and sped up the installations. Once that was taken car of, Pat and Dan were open for business five months before the competition. Their shop opened on a Thursday. That Saturday they serviced sixty-two vehicles.

Pat and Dan worked evenings and Saturdays at their store while maintaining their steel company jobs. Art, Jr. had graduated from Wabash College and, after two weeks of tutoring from Highland manager Bill Purnick, he went to work weekdays in the Calumet City Shop and Saturdays in South Holland. Even with his assistance it became clear to Pat and Dan that because of the fast growth, one of them would have to turn full time attention to their shop. Pat made the change and claims that she has never regretted it.

*Pat Tonkovich became the sole owner of a second Oil Express franchise in Chicago and was appointed Director of Operations for company stores.*

In 1984 I sold the first house where Connie and I had lived in Hammond on a thirty-year contract for $44,000 with a ten percent down payment. The payments are $350 per month with $3,500 per year applied toward the interest and $700 paying down the principal. Once the house is paid off, it will have netted us $144,000—an unbelievable profit for a $2,000 investment.

I thought back over my two recent unsuccessful partnerships and I could now see why they didn't work out. Both Nick and Dave had achieved success running their own businesses. It was only natural that they should want to control the new one. I needed someone younger—someone who hungered for an opportunity to make a lot of money and who would be willing to let me train him in the operation of the business. I had told Connie time and again that if I could just find five men who would listen to me, they could all be millionaires within five years.

At the time, CarX Muffler shops wanted me to merge with them and build forty CarX Oil Change stores. But again, I would not be in control, so I didn't seriously consider it. CarX did build one oil change shop near the Woodmar Shopping Center in Hammond. It was an excellent location but averaged only twenty cars per day.

After all my past disappointments, I began to wonder if I would ever find someone willing to learn from me. Everyone I'd dealt with seemed to be under the impression that if they received "X" amount of information, it was all they needed to proceed and succeed.

Since John Holloway's widow had put the management of his estate entirely in the hands of Jack Finnigan, her bank's trustee, Dan Barnes was under no obligation to her. I approached him with an offer. We listened to each other at length, stating our goals, and came to an agreement. Dan bought into the National Oil Express as a partner for a minute amount of money. I didn't care about the money—I wanted someone to work *with* me. I made certain that I kept the controlling interest. Dan understood that our possibilities as partners were vast.

It was a pleasure for me to work with an intelligent, open-minded person such as Dan; someone at my side who was not attempting to firmly grasp the lion's share of the business. Not all lawyers make successful businessmen, but Dan was an exception. Sometimes our meetings lasted through the night. Open minds and diligence beget rewards, it seems.

I am always looking for ways to build up the Oil Express name and I was very proud of Dan when he became president of Convenient Automotive Service Institute (CASI). Not only was Dan active in that capacity, but also as a participant in a road show with Joe Hazzard promoting the fast lube industry.

In 1985 my son John graduated from Hanover College and began training in the Highland Oil Express. He progressed rapidly and after nine months of learning all aspects of the oil change business, I was ready to give him his own store, delighted to have both sons involved in the company.

But John declined the offer. He talked with me at length, explaining that he did not feel his interest was in business but rather in furthering his education and pursuing his own dreams. I understood and supported his decision.

Meanwhile, Art, Jr.'s mechanical and technical deftness became indispensible in terms of opening new stores. His

*Art. Jr. conducting the monthly manager's meeting.*

responsibilities included overseeing the people who installed and set up the tanks which were connected to the buildings as well as coordinating the installation of the oil guns and related equipment. Then, once the shops were open, he'd work with the new franchisees and managers for two or three weeks. Each time this entire process took about two months. Art, Jr. was also in charge of managers' meetings, finding solutions to any technical problems, handling customer complaints and employee concerns. He contacted the auto manufacturers to prepare for the servicing of their vehicles for the new model year. On top of that this ambitious young man wrote the Lotus program at Oil Express headquarters to check monthly in-store accounting and the quarterly physical inventory analysis.

Everything began to click.

# Chapter 22
# Entrepreneur of the Year

*"If we had no winter, the spring*
*would not be so pleasant; if we did*
*not sometimes taste of adversity,*
*prosperity would not be so welcome."*

—*Anne Bradstreet*

Purdue University nominated me for the Entrepreneur of the Year Award in 1987 for the state of Indiana. The award was sponsored by Arthur Young and Venture Magazine. There were awards for the best of ten in seven categories. The Entrepreneur of the Year was the person with the best overall score for all the categories combined.

The black-tie ball was held in the Indiana Ballroom in Indianapolis with T. Boone Pickens as the evening's guest speaker. Connie and I went with a small entourage—Pat and Kathy Tonkovich, Art, Jr., and Judy Lebryk. Everyone in our little group was thrilled when I won in the category of Best

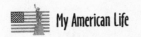 

Small Business Under Five Years Old.

Now it was time for the "Cinderella" of the awards—and there were many deserving nominees that year. We sat in silent anticipation, waiting for the announcement of the winner. The announcer leaned into the microphone..."Art Lukowski, Oil Express." Seven hundred people cheered...the *best business in the state*...I was overwhelmed. I made my way up to the stage and realized that for once I had lost my voice. As I took the award the only thing I managed to articulate was "God bless America."

While I was shaking hands and receiving congratulatory messages I noticed the familiar faces of Frank Steglich and Robert Lahey, two of my bankers from the Centier Bank in Highland. They had driven 125 miles to be there and had to return immediately after the festivities were over. I greatly appreciated their show of support—and still do. I shouldn't have been surprised. Centier was the most accommodating bank out of all those I had dealt with. That night was one of the happiest of my life. It was a validation, the culmination of a lifetime of experiences—the camps in Russia, the abduction of my father, life under the Nazis, my experiences in Scotland, my arrival in America, the restaurants, the long hours, the disappointments in the early years of Oil Express and the victories. They were all the things I had to experience to get me to this point.

The award was a real boon to business in the form of a great deal of free publicity. I was interviewed by newspapers in Illinois and Indiana along with several radio interviews. The combination of my accent and little formal education proved to be an inspiration to young people. They wanted to know my secret and I was happy to give them the information.

In that same year, Oil Express was voted one of the top ten businesses in Illinois by Arthur Anderson and the Small Business Administration. SCORE (Service Core of

178

Retired Executives) chose Oil Express as one of four out of more than three million businesses featured in their brochure which they used in the United States, Guam, and Puerto Rico.

Soon after, a Dr. Gerry Hill asked if I would speak at seminars designed for Eastern European business students coming to the United States to study. I agreed. I told them of my success with Oil Express and where they could go to get help, information, how to approach bankers, etc. I even gave some seminars to inmates in an Indiana prison, informing the young men how to seek a job and how to approach a prospective employer.

As the number of franchised and company owned stores increased, so did the need for staff members to help manage the company owned stores. Pat Tonkovich had opened her second Oil Express on Pulaski Road in Chicago, this time without a partner. She had also added two more bays to her shop in Calumet City, making it one of the few five bay fast lube shops in the country. Pat's sister, Kathy, helped run the two stores which gave Pat the time and the energy to become involved in the operation of the company stores. She worked with Art, Jr. which gave me a bit of relief and helped reduce the strain on our father-son relationship; a strain which had developed during our many months of working closely together. Pat became Director of Operations for Oil Express.

Another new and soon-to-be important person to appear on the Oil Express scene was Robert Sikorsky. Bob was a car care expert I'd met at a Convenient Automotive Service Institute (CASI) convention in Oklahoma. He'd written many books on the subject of car care, had articles published in *Reader's Digest*, and a syndicated column in national newspapers. I appointed him the Oil Express spokesperson.

In 1980 when the first Oil Express opened, one of the first technicians hired was Bill Purnick. Bill had gone on to supervise two Oil Express shops and to own and manage forty-nine percent of Turbo Car Wash with the other fifty-one percent belonging to my children. I was determined to make him management because of his willingness to learn—and learn he did. He eventually became one of the top managers in our organization and trained many company managers in the Highland store.

I've always felt it is important to share Oil Express's secrets of success with others in the industry,—even the competition. I believe that working together strengthens the entire industry and builds customer confidence in all of us.

Connie always said that my middle name was "Promotion" because of the value I place on advertising. Experience has shown me that it is necessary to replace seventeen percent of the customers of a business each year to replace those lost to relocation, retirement and a host of other reasons. Even with repeat customers a business needs new ones in order to grow. In keeping with this philosophy, Oil Express has participated in many festivals and parades, advertised in different ethnic newspapers and on radio and television. I also believe in giveaways such as calenders, apples, and so on. Two that proved to be the most fun took place in the South Holland store when I gave each customer an onion wrapped in mesh and tied with a bow. Another successful giveaway was a little flower that the cashier would stick on a customer's lapel. The onion,though—now *that* was a conversation piece. I knew that the combination of A-1 service and something to provide a chuckle or good feeling about having patronized your business to keep it in their memories was indeed a winning combination.

Until 1987 Dan and I had used our cars and rooms in our homes as offices. Dan had even produced a quarterly newsletter from his home. But the growth of the company necessitated the renting of office space and employing more office help. We moved Oil Express headquarters to Hinsdale, Illinois.

We enjoyed another bit of growth when we learned

how to purchase television time. We discovered that if we had our own advertising agency, we could hire professionals to create our own commercials. The Oil Express Advertising Agency was born.

It seemed that 1987 was a year for dreams to be actualized, but things suddenly took a turn for the worse. In July I underwent triple bypass heart surgery. I hadn't suffered a heart attack and the prognosis for a full recovery was excellent. Dr. Arie Dumanian, my friend as well as my surgeon, warned me to slow down in the business. This would be very difficult for me. The business was growing and I felt it had a long way to go. Not to be in charge of my small empire which took seven years to build was asking a lot.

During my period of recovery a major oil company made a tremendous offer to buy out Oil Express. It was an offer that merited serious consideration. While I was mulling it over Art, Jr., Dan and Pat suggested that, if I didn't sell, they would take on more responsibility in order to give me more time off. I took them up on their offer and turned down the oil company. I'd always intended to have my heirs inherit the company from their European patriarch.

The slowing down never happened. I did learn to pace myself well enough to be taken off my high blood pressure medication. Within two months of the surgery I attended the CASI convention in San Diego.

In 1988 I was inducted into the Entrepreneur Hall of Fame in Boca Raton, Florida. While returning from the ceremony I dictated a Code of Ethics for the fast lube business to Connie. It became the code for the entire industry and was later adopted by the CASI organization and shared with the members at their convention.

The years 1989 and 1990 were very productive for the company. In 1990, *National Lube and News* voted Joe Hazzard and I the Fast Lube Operators of the Year. While I was attending the World Trade Association at Purdue University I met Scott Williams, a consultant and Ivy Tech instructor. We had reached the point at Oil Express where we needed someone to better organize our training program. My biggest fear was losing the high standard of service that I had struggled to develop and maintain from that very first day back in 1980. There were hundreds of fine details in our system of customer service—some so subtle they went beyond the notice of the customer. I hired Scott and he worked with me for nine months to produce twenty-seven hours of training on nine video tapes, each three hours long. We then opened a training school in Chicago with classes kept to a student/teacher ration of fifteen to one. Once the project was complete, Scott became the advertising and marketing person for Oil Express.

At the next CASI convention I offered the training tapes free to anyone who wanted to use them. I was adamant about keeping the standard of service high throughout the industry. After six months I made the tapes available at cost plus shipping fees. Many of the Oil Express shops have a video tape machine in the basement where the tapes are played regularly as a refresher for the technicians. On our tapes we stress everything from telephone etiquette to a friendly goodbye for departing customers.

It all counts.

# Chapter 23

# Environmental Awareness

*"To the dull mind, all of nature is leaden. To the illumined mind, the whole world sparkles with light."*

—*Emerson*

George Chalos, my late chess partner and good, generous friend who had loaned Connie the $1000 when we were practically down to our last dime, had a son, Larry. Larry had met his wife when they were both employed at Art's Drive In some years back. Connie and I attended their wedding and even loaned them our brand new Buick with fewer than five hundred miles on the odometer when their car broke down and they were planning to cancel their honeymoon.

Larry was an enterprising individual who had acquired three liquor stores. He was also an accountant for the Lake County Mental Health Association. Being ambitious, Larry investigated many types of businesses. After considering many options, he purchased an Oil Express franchise. However, he wanted to open it up in Knoxville, Tennessee, because of the climate. I had always felt indebted to George for his generosity. Our families were good friends and I wanted to do anything I could to help Larry become successful. I called many oil companies to find out what I could about the

Knoxville area. The consensus was that, for the most part, people there liked to work on their own cars and the area wouldn't support a fast lube shop. The information was disheartening to Larry—so much so that I decided we should travel down there and investigate it ourselves.

On the first trip I noticed how busy the automatic car washes were. It seemed to me that if the people in Knoxville would not bother to wash their own cars, they probably wouldn't bother to change their own oil, either—especially if they had a convenient shop to go to. I approved of a location and Larry began construction of his own store. Once it was complete Art, Jr. went down to help him set up shop and get the business started. We had no way of knowing that our new franchisee would prove to be the most disappointing to date.

According to what Larry had told me, he intended to open several Oil Express stores in the Knoxville area. He did open more oil change shops—but not Oil Express shops. Larry didn't think that the company would learn about the other stores. When I confronted him, he claimed that he was running them for his mother. I knew this was pure fabrication. George and his wife had been our neighbors in both Hammond and Dyer. Mrs. Chalos was a widow and senior citizen and certainly not interested in the fast lube business.

The whole situation was a shame. Besides breaking his agreement Larry had fallen behind in his royalty payments. At least George was not around to see the problems Larry caused for me and Oil Express. The thought of taking my good friend's son to court hurt me very deeply. After many years of legal wrangling the matter was finally resolved in my favor.

In 1987, I bought out the CarX Oil Change shop that was still in operation near the Woodmar Mall in Hammond. Within two years, using the proven business methods and systems I developed for Oil Express, the car count went from twenty to seventy per day.

*The Highland Oil Express Turbo Wash complex.*

Six months later I bought several empty lots on the north and east sides of the Highland Oil Express. I couldn't tolerate them being vacant. I viewed them as canvasses—empty, before an artist brings them to life with a brush. And besides, all they were was a tax expense. I decided to develop a large car wash on the property which consisted of four automatic touchless wash bays and seven self-wash bays. As with the Oil Express stores, I took great pains to beautify the building and surrounding areas as well.

The first winter the Turbo Wash was open, my daughter, Lisa, a part-owner, became involved to get it running efficiently. The winter was particularly harsh and she had to wear a snowmobile suit in order to bear the brutal cold. In addition to helping out at the car wash and taking care of her eighteen-month and two-and-a-half year-old children, she helped out at the Hinsdale office part-time where she was learning various aspects of the Oil Express business.

*Lisa behind the counter of the
Highland Oil Express.*

While the Turbo Wash was under construction, I received another stern warning from my doctor to slow down. This time I took the advice more seriously. For a positive distraction, Connie and I bought a sixty-five foot yacht and aptly dubbed it *Work of Art*. We began spending some time away from the Chicago area, taking boat trips down the Mississippi, around to Florida, up the East coast and back. Connie felt that this was the perfect way to slow my pace down to one which would be conducive to good health. Every couple of months we would fly home so I could check the pulse of the business. The boat was a new adventure for both of us and effectively soothed the business beast within me.

*The* Work of Art.

During the four years from 1990 to 1993, Connie and I spent eight months of each of those years as terrors of the waters. We travelled 32,000 nautical miles, visited 280 ports in seventeen states and the Bahamas and Nassau. To date we've entertained more than 1,400 guests on our yacht.

I wasn't completely cut off from the business world while yachting. I kept up with several daily newspapers and business magazines and, during those months, read about oil spills and their effect on the environment. Preserving a healthy world has always been a concern of mine. Many of our Oil Express shops take used motor oil from do-it-yourselfers to prevent the oil from being dumped in the ground or disposed of with their trash. I became even more concerned when I read how massive illegal dumping had become. As a result I created the Help Save the World campaign which has

*The billboard in Highland, IN, which is part of the* Help Save the World *campaign begun by Art.*

since been joined by the Amoco Oil Company and Jiffy Lube. Lake County Indiana Solid Waste Management has published an outline of the campaign in its service magazine. If you drive down Indianapolis Boulevard in Highland you will see a beautiful world globe to remind each of us of our obligation to do what we can to "help save the world."

A changing of the guard occurred in October, 1993, when I appointed Dan Barnes President of Oil Express and Arthur, Jr. as its vice-president. Connie remained Director of the Board with Pat as Director of Operations. At last I felt confident that I family members in whom I could entrust my life's work.

*Art with new Oil Express President Dan Barnes.*

I once read the saying from old Burma Shave signs which read, "As you travel down life's highway, let always be your goal, to keep your eye upon the doughnut, and not upon the hole." I was determined to do this my entire life and now I feel truly blessed that God has allowed me and my family to partake in the rewards of that philosophy: health, wealth, and happiness.

I revel in a stimulating chess match with my son John. My soulmate Connie and I travel frequently—to Europe and CASI conventions and to visit other family members in the United States. My trips to Kiev have become an almost annual event.

# Chapter 24
## The Journey Back

*"Faith is the bird that feels the light
and sings when the dawn is still
dark."*

—*Rabindranath Tagores*

In 1990 something happened which was to change my focus and give me a new direction in my life.

The Governor of Indiana put together a group of six state senators and sixteen business people to go on a fact-finding mission to Eastern Europe. The purpose of this group was to determine how best to help the people of these countries help themselves after having lived under the thumb of tyrants for so many years and to also, if possible, develop trade for Indiana. I was honored to be included on this mission. We toured Poland, Hungary, Yugoslavia, and the former Soviet Union. Upon our return we reported our findings and recommendations to the state and federal governments. With my background and many visits there to my family over the years, I was confident recommending that hundreds of young people should be allowed to come to United States temporarily to be shown how a capitalistic system operates. These young people could be trained in our factories and offices since they had no clue as to how far behind the West they really were.

The response to my recommendation was negative.

Government people thought that by providing training for these young people it would seem as if they were taking jobs away from our own labor force. This was not my intent at all. They would only be here temporarily as observers and would then take their acquired knowledge and skills back home to build industries in their own countries. It was not to be.

I was disappointed that more couldn't be done to help in the business education of people in these emerging countries, so I decided to do what I could on my own. When I don't have any trips to Europe planned for myself, I bring someone here for two months to show them what life is like in the United States in the hope of inspiring them to accomplish something on their own.

I believe Eastern Europe to be a tremendous market waiting to be tapped. The people need everything from medical supplies and clothing to automotive parts and light bulbs—just about whatever Americans take for granted. Connie has heard me say many times, "If only I were ten years younger." At this point I can only dream of the many ventures begging to be explored and realized.

It was in that year of 1989 when I finally learned the fate of my father. The year before Gorbachev made the Soviet government open its archives to the public in reference to family members who had been arrested during the purges of Joseph Stalin. My niece, Anna, wrote to the general prosecutor in the Ukraine and we received a letter regarding the fate of my father.

Joseph Lukowski was not sent to Siberia. He was immured in the prison Zan had routinely visited, confined to an eight by twelve foot room with about a dozen other prisoners. There, they sat in silence. A single light bulb hung from the ceiling, never switched off in the name of Big-Brother-like observation. Each prisoner received a single bowl of grain per day. A concrete trough along one wall through which water ran continuously served as their toilet.

At intervals prisoners would be singled out and taken into an office where a confession and a pen were placed before him for his signature. Refusal meant being returned to the cell. Usually after a few weeks the prisoner would sign. With no hope of being released unless they did so, the thought of going back to the cell with no room to lie down or move around caused them to relinquish their integrity and sign—if for nothing more than the thought of being able to stretch and breathe fresh air. Evidently my father was among those who resisted the longest before signing—he endured nearly ten months in that cell.

We also learned from the letter that whenever guards said a person would be "sent to Siberia for ten years with no communication," they always meant "Death." If they said, "Sent to Siberia" without adding "no communication," it meant "sent to Siberia."

And so it was for father. He had been arrested on December 4, 1937 and executed—shot—on September 20, 1938.

Records from the archives revealed that he was actually convicted of passing blueprints of bridges and roads to Polish scouts, thereby committing acts of treason according to three military judges. In 1990 the case of Joseph Lukowski was reviewed and, since there was no evidence to support the charges, he was granted a pardon—fifty-two years too late. Poor mother died under the assumption that he had perished in Siberia with millions of Stalin's other victims.

I learned that father was buried in Bykovnya Woods near Kiev in a mass grave containing the bodies of 150,000 registered victims. No one knows for certain how many non-registered victims are buried there as well. Some experts estimate that there are over 700,000 at this site alone. Anywhere from 25 to 150 people per day were executed and buried there during the Soviet Holocaust from 1917 through 1953, which took about 40 million lives. From 1932 to 1938 alone, 11 million Ukrainians died from being starved or executed. The truth has been hidden for so long that no one will ever know the full magnitude of the once open-armed Ukraine. The truth is voiceless, just as the carnate themselves became.

I booked air passage to the Ukraine to pay my respects to my father—to finally say the farewell that was in my heart when the opportunity to voice it was stolen by the soldiers in 1937.

The Bykovnya Woods gravesite, the resting place of a population, was badly neglected. The site had been a "dirty little secret" of the Soviets for decades, the people within as enslaved by their shroud of neglect in death just as they had been by Stalin in life. They were devoid of human care and visitors. It deeply saddened me to realize that my father's remains were confined in a setting that lacked the warmth which was so characteristic of him in life; a setting which lacked even a small portion of the respect due to him.

In October, 1992, National Geographic photographers pictured this tired pine grove, the only evidence of the people buried there being a few rough cardboard markers wired to individual tree trunks. It reminded me of Mary Magdelene, sorrowful in her rags. It was then that I decided that these victims must have a voice.

I had Anna phone the Ukraine National Television to inform them of my intention to arrive on September 26, 1994, bearing one thousand roses for my father and the other voiceless victims, their faces only existing now in the memories of their family members—family members with whom I empathized.

That day Art, Jr. and I led an automobile procession of relatives through the woods. The midday sun filtered through the pine boughs as the headlights of the cars behind gleamed in the rearview mirror. We finally stopped and walked up to the small, unworthy monument. A giant wreath of red roses

## Images of Bykovnya

*(Clockwise from top) Art holds a flag, flanked by two Russian patriot soldiers who spent twenty years in prison.*

*Priests bless the monument.*

*Statue of the Ukrainian worker.*

*Art locates his father's paper marker on a tree.*

*Art shakes hands with the mayor of Kiev.*

connected the statue with the small wooden cross, and surrounded a fading photograph of my father. With tears in my
eyes, I bent to kiss the picture. Art, Jr. wept for a grandfather
he will never know. Other people lay their wreaths and flowers at the monument and we all join in a group prayer.

The visit was televised throughout the Ukraine and
reported in Ukrainian newspapers. Seven months later I
accepted an invitation to attend the first public memorial for
the victims.

And so here I stand. The silent prayer begins once
again, its silence bringing forth a tone louder than any funeral dirge. When it is finished, the priests sprinkle holy water on
the memorial and the uniformed patriot soldiers in attendance—soldiers who spent twenty years behind Stalin's iron
bars. I turn as the holy men then light the candles and look
up at the monument. The man in the monument is my father.
He is also the father, the son, the brother, the uncle, the
cousin, the grandfather, the nephew of the millions of people
whose home was part of the U.S.S.R. He is the one who
would never return to them.

Only one out of four did return from the war. Only
one out of seven returned from the prisons of Siberia. Millions
never did.

The base of the monument is
inscribed:

> *Dearest is freedom.*
> *We die for it.*

# Epilogue

*"Gratitude is memory of the heart."*
—Massieu

Today Art's family and ten of his franchisees are millionaires. Although successful, there are many other priceless, more important benefits and gifts they've received over the years.

Art once said to Connie, "I could own a bridge." But he doesn't. He and Connie live comfortably in their Dyer, Indiana neighborhood surrounded by people they've grown to care about, within a community whose members they respect and where they feel welcome.

Besides Lisa's children, Jill and Ben, now in Virginia, Art, Jr. and his wife Susan have blessed them with two grand-daughters, Danielle and Caitlin. John, unmarried, is a psychologist and lives in Minnesota. To Art and Connie they are all life's greatest joy.

Art feels lucky to have found two of his three brothers alive after the war—so many millions found no one and were left alone. He feels fortunate that he and his dear mother, Josephine, survived the Nazi labor camp.

"It was even fortunate to have been placed in that

# Epilogue

Connie

Arthur, jr.

John

Lisa

The grandchildren
(from left to right):
Danielle, Jill, Ben,
and Caitlin

*Art at the podium the night he received the Lifetime Achievement Award at the Conrad Hilton Towers in Chicago in November, 1996.*

*The Lukowski Home in Dyer, Indiana.*

labor camp; without it, I would still be entangled in the after-effects of communist beliefs," Arthur says. "Most of all, I feel blessed to have been able to overcome the obstacles I faced in Europe and America with only four years of formal education."

Although his accent still hints of his European lineage and made for a rough entry into the restaurant business, he has shown through his example that language and formal education are not the only factors in the equation of success. He is indeed grateful for each and every person he met along his path to success who gave him a reason to hope.

Art has continued his search for information about his father and his extended family. With the help of the Society of Fellows of Political Victims of Repression during a May, 1996 visit to the Ukraine, he was able open his father's file and given permission to copy some of the documents by hand. This included six pages of transcripts of the interrogation of Joseph which listed the names of three witnesses against him, two of which were known to the Lukowski family. Art was also able to get photocopies of his father's arrest order

*A copy of the document confirming that*
*Joseph had been executed as ordered.*

УКРАЇНА
ПОНОВЛЕНО

## СВІДОЦТВО ПРО СМЕРТЬ

Громадянин (ка) **Луковський**
**Йосип    Іванович**
помер (ла) **21 вересня 1938 року**
**двадцять першого вересня тисяча дев"ятсот**
**тридцять восьмого року**
у віці **46** років, про що в книзі реєстрації актів про смерть
19 **96** року **червня** місяця **28** числа
зроблено запис за № **7**
Причина смерті **Розстріл**

Місце смерті: місто, селище **Невідомо**

район

область

держава

Місце реєстрації **відділ реєстрації актів громадян-**
**ського стану Дніпровського району м.Києва**
Дата видачі **28 червня** 19 **96** р.

М. П.

Завідуючий відділом запису
актів громадянського стану

І-БК № 189328

ПК «Українка» 3-4870 1993. IV.

*The copy of Joseph's Death Certificate which was given to Art.*

dated 12/3/37; the protocol of the arrest at which time the
soldier's took forty-four of the family's photos (none
remained in the file); two passports of Josepha Lukowska;

eight I.D.'s for Joseph Lukowski; documentation of a 5/30/38 interrogation where the interrogator asked for a month's more time for Joseph (two other interrogators agreed); the order for Joseph to be shot; and a document confirming that he had been shot.

One of the I.D.'s named Joseph's birthplace. Arthur flew from Kiev to Vilnos where he rented a car with a chauffeur. They drove to the village of Klykoliai where they found two people who knew of the Lukowskis. Art learned that his father came from a family of ten children—six sons and four daughters. The sons were Zan, Henry, Jone, August, Jozeph and Fricic; the daughters were Minnie, Emilia, Darja and Natalja. The two people knew two of the sons, Art's uncles Zan and Henry. They explained that some Lukowski graves were in a forest in Latvia but to get there Art would have to cross the border at another location. The driver suggested they try the bridge at Klykoliai.

When they arrived they encountered four armed guards. Art asked one of them if he and his driver might cross into Latvia to search the cemetery for the graves of relatives. The guard walked over to a Latvian guard who turned out to be very friendly and gave the driver directions to the cemetery, about three-quarters of a mile away.

At the cemetery Art discovered that about eighty percent of the graves were unmarked. He was about to admit defeat and call it a day when a car pulled up and an elderly gentlemen got out. Art asked if he knew where they might go to find information about the location of the Lukowski family graves.

"Follow me," he told him and led them to five graves. They had been overlooked by Art because the names on the markers were written in Latvian, unrecognizable to him. Surprisingly, one of the graves had been recently tended to with fresh flowers. The marker bore the name of Emilia Lukowski, 1885-1972.

Back in the village Art could find no other information, so he traveled to the County Register Office where a wonderful lady searched the records for more than an hour and finally located the name of a woman who was most likely a relative of Art's.

Art went to the address given to him at the Register Office and introduced himself to a lady named Wilma who lived with her husband and son, also named Arthur. Wilma pulled out her photos. Some of them were of Art's family in Boston—the Bergs and Aunt Emily who had sponsored him on his entry into America in 1954. Art also learned of another living relative, the daughter of his recently discovered aunt Natalja. Wilma told them that her family had been sent to Siberia in 1948. Her father died there. She and her mother were given permission to return to Latvia in 1960, but with no money or help to get there from Siberia.

A death certificate was finally issued for Joseph in July, 1996. Of forty-seven documents originally contained in Joseph's file, two were missing. One was of particular interest because it most likely listed the name of Joseph's accuser. A neighbor? A member of the Central Committee? Who?

Arthur intends to keep searching until he finds out.